CAMBRIDGE LIBRARY COLLECTION

Books of enduring scholarly value

Perspectives from the Royal Asiatic Society

A long-standing European fascination with Asia, from the Middle East to China and Japan, came more sharply into focus during the early modern period, as voyages of exploration gave rise to commercial enterprises such as the East India companies, and their attendant colonial activities. This series is a collaborative venture between the Cambridge Library Collection and the Royal Asiatic Society of Great Britain and Ireland, founded in 1823. The series reissues works from the Royal Asiatic Society's extensive library of rare books and sponsored publications that shed light on eighteenth- and nineteenth-century European responses to the cultures of the Middle East and Asia. The selection covers Asian languages, literature, religions, philosophy, historiography, law, mathematics and science, as studied and translated by Europeans and presented for Western readers.

A Translation of the Memoirs of Eradut Khan

A nobleman of the court of the Mughal emperor, Iradat Khan (*c.*1649–1716) experienced the rule of Aurangzeb (1618–1707) and observed at first hand the decline of the Mughal empire. This English translation of his memoirs was first published in 1786 by Jonathan Scott (1754–1829), a captain of the East India Company. He translated Khan's memoirs in order to educate the British about India's history and inform them about the Mughal empire. In these memoirs Khan relates anecdotes of his encounters with Aurangzeb and recounts the events following the emperor's death, including the rule of his son Bahadur Shah (1643–1712) between 1707 and 1712. The memoirs conclude with the death of Jahandar Shah (1661–1713), who ruled only briefly before being beaten in battle, captured and executed. Also included are extracts from Aurangzeb's last letters.

T0382608

Cambridge University Press has long been a pioneer in the reissuing of out-of-print titles from its own backlist, producing digital reprints of books that are still sought after by scholars and students but could not be reprinted economically using traditional technology. The Cambridge Library Collection extends this activity to a wider range of books which are still of importance to researchers and professionals, either for the source material they contain, or as landmarks in the history of their academic discipline.

Drawing from the world-renowned collections in the Cambridge University Library and other partner libraries, and guided by the advice of experts in each subject area, Cambridge University Press is using state-of-the-art scanning machines in its own Printing House to capture the content of each book selected for inclusion. The files are processed to give a consistently clear, crisp image, and the books finished to the high quality standard for which the Press is recognised around the world. The latest print-on-demand technology ensures that the books will remain available indefinitely, and that orders for single or multiple copies can quickly be supplied.

The Cambridge Library Collection brings back to life books of enduring scholarly value (including out-of-copyright works originally issued by other publishers) across a wide range of disciplines in the humanities and social sciences and in science and technology.

A Translation of
the Memoirs
of Eradut Khan

A Nobleman of Hindostan,
Containing Interesting Anecdotes
of the Emperor Aulumgeer Aurungzebe,
and of his Successors

TRANSLATED BY JONATHAN SCOTT

CAMBRIDGE
UNIVERSITY PRESS

CAMBRIDGE UNIVERSITY PRESS

Cambridge, New York, Melbourne, Madrid, Cape Town,
Singapore, São Paolo, Delhi, Mexico City

Published in the United States of America by Cambridge University Press, New York

www.cambridge.org
Information on this title: www.cambridge.org/9781108055130

© in this compilation Cambridge University Press 2013

This edition first published 1786
This digitally printed version 2013

ISBN 978-1-108-05513-0 Paperback

A

TRANSLATION

OF THE

MEMOIRS OF ERADUT KHAN,

A NOBLEMAN OF HINDOSTAN,

CONTAINING

INTERESTING ANECDOTES

OF THE

EMPEROR AULUMGEER AURUNGZEBE,

AND OF HIS SUCCESSORS,

SHAW AULUM AND JEHAUNDAR SHAW;

IN WHICH ARE DISPLAYED

THE CAUSES OF THE VERY PRECIPITATE DECLINE,

OF THE

MOGUL EMPIRE IN INDIA.

———————

By JONATHAN SCOTT,

CAPTAIN IN THE SERVICE OF THE HONOURABLE EAST-INDIA COMPANY,
AND PRIVATE PERSIAN TRANSLATOR TO WARREN HASTINGS, ESQUIRE,
LATE GOVERNOR-GENERAL OF BENGAL, &c. &c. &c.

———————

LONDON:

PRINTED FOR JOHN STOCKDALE, OPPOSITE BURLINGTON-HOUSE, PICCADILLY.
MDCCLXXXVI.

TO

WARREN HASTINGS, Esq.

SIR,

PERMIT me to dedicate this Tranflation to you, who fo amply patronized my attempts to make myfelf ufeful to my honourable employers, when in India. The diftinction you were pleafed to confer upon me, by an appointment in your family, and the favour of your friendfhip, I fhall ever regard as honours of which I may reafonably boaft: and I truft a time will come, when far more important pages than mine will acquire merit with the nation, from being adorned with the name of HASTINGS.

I am, SIR,

Your moft obedient

And grateful humble fervant,

LONDON,
12th May, 1786.

JONATHAN SCOTT.

E R R A T A.

Page

29, line 20, *for* meſſuage, *read* meſſage.

30, line 24, *for* Raujepoet, *read* Raujpoot.

51, line 2, in the notes, *for* mizid, *read* muzjid.

52, line 10, *for* Bahadar, *read* Bahadur.

54, line 2, *for* Soubadacy, *read* Soubadary.

83, in the notes, *for* Yemmum, *read* Yemmun.

89, line 8, *and* 22, *for* Downan, *and* Dowran, *read* Dowraun.

PREFACE.

ENcouraged by the generous attention of my honour-able mafters, the Eaft-India Company, and of their reprefentatives in Bengal, to every fpecies of ufeful information from their fervants, I was induced, during my refidence in India, to ftudy the languages and hiftory of the country, with a view of recommending myfelf to their notice and favour. I alfo cherifhed the hope of lay-ing up a fund of amufement from thefe ftudies for the hours of retirement, fhould I be fo fortunate as to revifit my native country : nor was I without the ambition, of being able to add fomewhat to the ftore of public informa-tion refpecting the extenfive empire of Hindoftan, of which Great-Britain poffeffes fo large a fhare. Rewarded by the accomplifhment of my two firft objects, I am now led to try the merit of the laft.

The Hiftory of Hindoftan, from the earlieft Mahum-medan conquefts to the year 1669 of our æra, has been already prefented to the public by the late Colonel Dow, who, had he lived, would in all probability have continued

it

it down to the prefent day ; but, unfortunately, his work concludes at a period, when the affairs of Hindoftan were becoming moft interefting to European curiofity. I mean the 11th year of Aulumgeer, commonly called Aurungzebe, the events of whofe reign, and thofe of his fucceffors, are to us more important, as nearer to our own times.

The celebrated Mr. Orme, when writing of this period in his Hiftorical Fragments of Hindoftan, regrets the want of information regarding it, and juftly obferves, " the " knowledge is well worth the enquiry ; for, befides the " magnitude of the events, and the energy of the cha- " racters, which arife in this period, there are no ftates " or powers on the continent of India, with whom our " nation have either connexion or concern, who do not " owe their prefent condition to the reign of Aurungzebe, " or to its influence on the reigns of its fucceffors."

It is the Hiftory of Dekkan, and the above-mentioned very important period, with which, if the following Tranflation is approved, I hope fhortly to prefent the public. Of materials I have no want, but muft confefs myfelf unwilling to labour in their arrangement, without fome profpect of fuch a tafk's proving acceptable. On this account, I have judged it prudent to offer firft a fpecimen of my work, that, if unworthy of the public eye, I may keep the remainder of it in that privacy I fhall then think

it

it only fit for, and fave myfelf the pain of difappointed expectation.

The following Memoir is tranflated from the Perfic of Eradut Khan, a nobleman of the court of Aulumgeer. The authenticity of the facts he relates is undoubted in Hindoftan, and the fimplicity of his ftyle regarded as a ftrong proof of his veracity. I have ftudioufly endeavoured to make him write Englifh, in the fame unaffected and plain manner that he has his native tongue; being more anxious for the fidelity of my tranflation, than defirous of praife for compofition.

It now remains only to give a fhort introduction to the fubject of my author. It is generally known, that the Emperor Aulumgeer reigned fifty years over Hindoftan, and extended his empire, before too vaft to be fecure, over the fouthern peninfula of India, called Dekkan, in the reduction of which he fpent the laft five-and-twenty years of his life. In this period, he reduced the monarchies of Golconda and Beejapore; but though he could conquer enervated kings, he could not fubdue the minds of their uncorrupted fubjects. His zeal for the Mahummedan religion, led him to deprive the Hindoo princes of thofe indulgences which his lefs bigotted anceftors had allowed them : he deftroyed their temples, and difgraced them by a capitation-tax. This tyranny weakened the affections of the

ancient

ancient vaffals of the houfe of Timur, and raifed fuch a fpirit of refiftance in the hardy natives of Dekkan that could never be effectually fubdued. Sewajee and his fucceffors, the Mharatta chiefs, though they could not wholly withftand the Imperial arms, yet fo harraffed Aulumgeer by their predatory incurfions, as to render his victories of no advantage. The treafures of the old provinces were diffipated in half-conquefts of new territory, and the emperor's long abfence from his hereditary dominions, occafioned a univerfal weaknefs in the powers of government. The nobility and army, tired with nearly thirty years of conftant war, were grown remifs, and anxious for repofe in the luxurious pleafures of Dhely and Agra. Aurungzebe's three fons, ambitious of empire, waited only the death of their father, to fight againft each other for the important prize. Thus every circumftance combined to bring on the decline of the Mogul empire, and involve it in the miferies related by Eradut Khan, whom I fhall now leave to fpeak for himfelf.

ORIGINAL

ORIGINAL

P R E F A C E.

THUS fayeth the compiler of thefe records and events, an humble and finful flave, ¹Moobaric Oollah ²Eradut Khan Wazeh, fon of the ⁴ fheltered in mercy, ⁵Keffaiut Khan, writer of the ⁶Shekeft: When I had finifhed the ⁷Kulmaut Aleeaut, it entered my mind to draw up a concife relation of what events had happened to myfelf, while I was compofing that work.

---

¹ Anglicè, Bleffed of God.

² The author's title of nobility, fignifying The Faithful Lord.

³ His poetical name, by which he chofe to fignify himfelf in his poems; Anglicè, Clear. Eaftern authors always ufe one.

⁴ The Muffulmauns, when mentioning a deceafed perfon, never fay fuch a one who is dead, but fuch a one fheltered in mercy, received in pardon, or fome fimilar expreffion. When mentioning a deceafed prince, they fay the prince whofe feat is in Paradife.

⁵ Anglicè, The ferviceable.

⁶ The broken hand, generally ufed in bufinefs.

⁷ Anglicè, Sublime Difcourfes. This work I never could obtain, though I made ftrict enquiry after it.

I have

I have obferved, that delightful fcenes, and the fociety of friends, are not fo ftriking at the time of enjoyment, as afterwards, when reflected in the mirror of recollection. On this account, I write down moft paffing occurrences; and whenever I perufe them, or ruminate upon them, a particular feeling, a furprifing pleafure and aftonifhing extafy, prevail in my mind. My writings alfo ferve as a memorial to my friends.

During the fhort period of my age, which has this day arrived at the fixty-fourth year, and the 1126th of the holy A.C. 1715. Hijhera, fuch wonders of time, fuch aftonifhing marks of the power of the Creator of night and day in the viciffi-tudes of worldly affairs, the deftruction of empires, the deaths of many princes, the ruin of ancient houfes and noble families, the fall of worthy men, and rife of the unworthy, have been beheld by me, as have not been mentioned by hiftory to have occurred, in fuch number or fucceffion, in a thoufand years.

As, on account of my office, and being engaged in thefe tranfactions, I have obtained a perfect knowledge of the fources of moft events, and what, to others, even in-formation of muft be difficult, was planned and executed in my fight; and as I was a fharer, as well as fpectator,

of

of all the dangers and troubles, I have therefore recorded them.

My intention, however, not being to compile a hiftory of kings, or a flowery work, but only to relate fuch events as happened within my own knowledge, I have therefore, preferably to a difplay of learning in lofty phrafes and pompous metaphors, chofen a plain ftyle, fuch as a friend, writing to a friend, would ufe for the purpofe of information. Indeed, if propriety is confulted, loftinefs of ftyle is unfit for plain truth, which, pure in itfelf, requires only a fimple delineation. I hope, therefore, that my readers will not loofen the reins of impartiality from their hands, nor call my modefty, ignorance.

TO

TO THE

R E A D E R.

IT will be neceffary to remember, that Aurungzebe is the fame perfon with Aulûmgeer. He took the latter title on his acceffion to the throne, agreeable to the cuftom of the eaftern princes, who always affume a new one on that occafion.

It is hoped that the number of notes will not prove tedious, nor perplex the reader's attention. Some, perhaps, may appear trivial to thofe whofe local knowledge renders fuch affiftance, to them, unneceffary; but, as their number is comparatively very fmall with thofe who require it, the tranflator requefts the indulgence of the few, in compliment to the many.

MEMOIRS

MEMOIRS

OF THE

MOGUL EMPIRE,

BY

ERADUT KHAN WAZEH.

I SHALL begin my narration from the time of my removal from the command of the fortress of [1] Imteeauz Gur. For the duties of that office I had entertained numerous followers, a tenth of a tenth of whom, the suddenness of my recall rendered me incapable of paying; but, as my life was yet to remain, I made my [2] escape from among them in the best manner I could, with my family.

On account of my distressed circumstances, and the great distance of my late command from the Imperial camp, in order that I

---

[1] An important fortress in Dekkan, or the southern part of Hindostan. It is called Oodneh by the Hindoos, and is now in possession of the Mharattas, who retook it soon after the death of the Emperor Aulumgeer.

[2] To be obliged to fly from their own troops, is frequently the case with the nobles of Hindostan, on recall from office, or other emergency, as they generally keep up more than they can pay with regularity.

B   might

might take fome repofe, his majefty had conferred upon me the government of [1] Ahffunabad Koolburgah, where I remained one month; and then, leaving my deareft fon, [2] Huddaiut Oolla, as my deputy in that ftation, I proceeded with a few followers to the [3] Stirrup. I had the honour of an audience in [4] Pargur, while his majefty was engaged in the reduction of [5] Kundaneh. He fhewed me much favour, nor had any change taken place in his efteem and regard towards me. I was ftationed, during the fiege, four cofs diftant from the camp, on the only road of communication then left, as I had been fuccefsfully employed on the like fervice, fince the commencement of the reduction of Dekkan, at [6] Beejapore, [7] Hyderabad, and other places. Though the enemy now was very numerous, and plundered even to the fkirts of the camp, yet, by the divine affiftance, I maintained my poft with a very trifling force. For this fervice, I was honoured with much applaufe by his majefty, and my reputation with the public became high. Additional rank was alfo conferred, as a reward, on my deareft fon, and other relations, at Koolburgah.

---

[1] A city, formerly the capital of the Bhamenee fovereigns of Dekkan, Ferifhta's Hiftory of whom, and the fucceeding Dynafties, has been tranflated, and will one day be offered to the public, fhould their approbation await this attempt. It is now of little note, and in poffeffion of the Nizam.

[2] Anglicè, directed by God.

[3] Meaning the emperor's perfon, when travelling.

[4] A fortrefs in Dekkin.

[5] Another in ditto.

[6] Once the capital of the Adil Shawee Sultans of Dekkan, and celebrated for its magnificence. It was reduced by Aulumgeer, with all the dependencies, except what the famous Mharatta chief, Sewajee, who was a rebellious vaffal of this monarchy, had wrefted from it. It is now ruined, and in poffeffion of the Mharattas. Europeans have generally written it Vifiapour, but the Muffulmauns as above.

[7] This city was the capital of Golconda and Koottub Shawee fultans, the laft of whom was taken prifoner by Aulumgeer, and his kingdom reduced. It is now one of the capitals of the Nizam, who is however obliged to fhare the revenues with the Mharattas.

3   After

After the reduction of [1] Kundaneh and [2] Raujegur, the emperor moved to another quarter. He had defired feveral of the principal nobility to accept the command of the latter, as it was of importance, and but newly conquered; but it being a poft only of difficulty, they had all requefted to be excufed. One evening therefore he fent for me, and my fon [3] Moraud Khan, and when I had entered the prefence, faid, " I wifh to fend thee to Raujegur, art " thou willing to go ? " I replied, that his flave was ready; upon which he gave me part of the coffee before him, and ordered that, having drank it in the [4] Aubdar Khauneh, I fhould come back, and receive my difmiffion. When I returned to the prefence, his majefty gave me his bleffing, two hundred mhors, and one coin weighing one hundred [5] mhors, with two horfes to me and my fon, and five for my bretheren. Two hundred bullock loads of grain were alfo ordered with me; and the following day, after morning prayer, I departed. At taking leave, his majefty promifed that I fhould be relieved before the rainy feafon, then about two months diftant.

By the aufpices of the divine bleffing, I arrived in fafety at my ftation in eight days, and remained there forty; during which, from the folitude and romantic fituation of the place, my leifure paffed in pleafingly enthufiaftic contemplation. [6] Munfoor Khan was
then

---

[1] A fortrefs in Dekkan.

[2] Another in ditto.

[3] Anglicè, object of defire.

[4] The place in which water, fherbets, &c. are cooled in ice or faltpetre.

[5] Golden coins, of this and greater weight, were often given as marks of favour. Silver coins, of feveral hundred rupees value, were alfo in ufe; and there is one of them now in the Britifh Mufeum, of which the ingenious Mr. Richardfon has given a very full defcription, in his very learned work, the Perfian and Arabic Dictionary.

[6] Victorious. It is, perhaps, not yet quite unneceffary to mention, that every proper name or title of perfons, in the Perfian, and frequently in the Hindoo language,

is

then sent to relieve me, and his majesty wrote with his own hand on the firmaun of recall, that, agreeably to his promise, he commanded me to the presence; to which were added many gracious assurances of favour. I left Raujegur with the same force I had come; but as it was a great distance from the camp, and parties of the enemy were hovering abroad, at several places I was much pressed. On my arrival at the presence, I was received with great favour.

Being now again in the same situation as when I quitted Imteeauz Gur, (for my jagheer had been ruined by various depredations,) I was much distressed in my affairs, when his majesty, who was informed of every thing public and private, sent [1] Ameer Khan to me with a message, importing, that, as distress had invaded my affairs, I had better seek a little repose in some settled office, and that he would confer upon me the [2] Kelladaree and [3] Fojedaree of [4] Mandou, then held by [5] Nowazush Khan, who, though an ameer of three thousand, was unequal to the post.

My attachment and regard to his majesty were so great, that, observing his life verging to the close, I did not wish to quit the

---

is an epithet descriptive of some quality in them on whom it is conferred, or the donor supposes them to possess: but, of late years, titles of honour are become so common, as to lose their respect; and there are many victorious lords of Hindostan, who never saw a battle, or drew a sword against an enemy.

[1] Noble.
[2] Command of a garrison.
[3] Military authority in a district, under which are the criminal courts of justice.
[4] A very extensive fortress in the province of Malwa, of which it was the capital under the Patan sovereigns. It is now much decayed, and in possession of the Mharattas.
[5] Possessing affability.

prefence, fearful of never beholding him more, and therefore declined the offer; but, when my fon and the women of my family heard of the refufal, they became immerfed in grief, for the Soubah of Malwa was to them dear as their native place. The difappointment of my fon was fuch, that he privately refolved to give up the fervice, and leave me; and my whole family were heartlefs and in defpair. At length, overcome by their fituation, and indeed they had juftice on their fide, I, in fpite of my own grief, faid to my fon, " The power is in thy hands; I refign myfelf as a ranfom for " thy happinefs." The foul of my life went the fame evening to Ameer Khan, and informed him of my acceptance of this office. As that minifter was pleafed with my confenting on many accounts, he reprefented it to the emperor the fame night, when the affair was fettled. Alas! how can I exprefs what paffed within my own breaft? The following morning, at the affembly of juftice, his majefty beftowed upon me a horfe and ² khelaut, and the fame upon my fon and grandfon. It was alfo allowed me, at my particular requeft, to come daily to pay my refpects at the prefence, till the grants of my new office could be prepared; and though my pofts of ³ Meer Tozuk and ⁴ Darogah of the Dekkan cavalry were given to others, yet, from his majefty's gracious favor, I was permitted to exercife the duties of them till I left the camp.

---

¹ It was a cuftom of the Mogul emperors to fit daily once, for the purpofe of hearing and redreffing the complaints of the people, and often twice; but this noble ufage was difcontinued by the fucceffors of Aulumgeer, which tended greatly to lofe them the refpect of their fubjects.

² An honorary drefs given always to perfons entering into office, and frequently by a fuperior to an inferior, as a mark of efteem. It is varied, in richnefs of materials, and number of garments, according to the rank of the receiver.

³ A marfhal, whofe bufinefs it is to preferve order in a proceffion, or line of march, and to report abfentees.

⁴ Superintendant, who examines the number of men and horfes, to check falfe mufters.

On

On the evening before my departure, the emperor opening the window of his sleeping apartment, called me to him, and said, " Absence now takes place between us, and our meeting again is " uncertain. Forgive, then, whatever willingly, or unwillingly, " I may have done against thee, and pronounce the words, *I* " *forgive!* three times, with sincerity of heart. As thou hast " served me long, I also forgive thee whatever knowingly, or other- " wise, thou mayest have done against me." Upon hearing these expressions, my sobs became like a knot in my throat, so that I had not power to speak. At last, after his majesty had repeatedly pressed me, I made shift to pronounce the words, *I forgive!* three times, interrupted by heavy sobs. He shed many tears, repeated the words, and, after blessing me, ordered me to retire. Sorrow lay so heavy upon my mind, that, upon my arrival at ¹ Aurunga-bad, I was seized with a violent illness ; but, as my borrowed life was not yet required, the soul and body did not separate. Until my arrival at Mandou, I was unable to move, without help, from my bed to my feat. My son remained in the fort with me only one night, and then departed for his command at ² Koterree Perrayeh. I remained one year immersed in the same grief and sorrow.

The prince Mahummud ³ Bedar Bukht being appointed to the government of Malwa, I paid my respects to him at ⁴Oojein. In

---

¹ A considerable city, founded by Aulumgeer before his accession to the throne, near the celebrated fortrefs of Dowlutabad in Dekkan. He named it Khojefteh Boonniaud, or The Happy Mansion ; but the people called it Aurungabad, in com-pliment to his title of Aurungzebe, by which Aulumgeer was distinguished before he seized the empire.

² A district in Malwa.

³ Signifying wakeful star, or propitious fortune. He was the eldest son of Azim Shaw.

⁴ Supposed to be one of the oldest cities in India, and is at present the capital of Malwa, and of Mahajee Sindia, a principal Mharatta chief.

a short

a fhort time, fuch a friendfhip grew between us, that a greater between a prince and fubject cannot be conceived. He would not be an inftant without me: he would not eat of any thing, but he fent me part of it: he did nothing of importance without afking my advice, and confidered my opinion as religioufly decifive. In fhort, the particulars of his favour are beyond relation; but, on this account, I became envied by all his dependants.

Soon after this, the illuftrious prince Mahummud ¹ Azim Shaw, coming from Guzarat to vifit the emperor, paffed through Malwa, on his route to ² Ahmednuggur. From the favour he had beheld me in with his father, my attention to himfelf, and the unbounded praifes of his fon Bedar Bukht, he behaved to me in fuch a gracious manner, as to relate would occafion prolixity. When he had gone through Malwa, the government of Guzarat was conferred on Bedar Bukht, who departed for that province,. and took me with him as far as the frontiers, beyond which I dared not pafs without leave from the emperor. How fhall I exprefs his manner of part-ing? He made me promife to write him weekly, and faid, that he would favour me as often with letters under his own hand, in-cluding every important occurrence, in order to have the benefit of my advice for his conduct. This fort of correfpondence was kept up between us regularly, till the life of his majefty fhadow ³ of God arrived at an end. I muft now relate fome particulars of that important event ⁴.

A.H. 1118.
A.C. 1707,
Feb. 21ft.

The

---

¹ Signifying great king. He was the third by birth, but fecond furviving fon of Aulumgeer.

² A confiderable city of Dekkan, once the capital of the Nizam Shawee fultans, reduced to the Mogul yoke under Shaw Jehaun, but now under the Mharattas.

³ An epithet common to majefty, with all the orientals.

⁴ It may not be amifs to infert here two letters written by Aulumgeer to his fons, Azim Shaw and Kaum Bukfh, a few days before his death.

To

The emperor, a few days before his death, with a ſtrictneſs of command ſeldom to be enforced by monarchs at ſuch a ſeaſon, diſpatched

To Shaw Azim Shaw.

HEALTH to thee! My heart is near thee. Old age is arrived : weakneſs ſubdues me, and ſtrength has forſaken all my members. I came a ſtranger into this world, and a ſtranger I depart. I know nothing of myſelf, what I am, and for what I am deſtined. The inſtant which paſſed in power, hath left only ſorrow behind it. I have not been the guardian and protector of the empire. My valuable time has been paſſed vainly. I had a patron in my own dwelling, (conſcience,) but his glorious light was unſeen by my dim ſight. Life is not laſting; there is no veſtige of departed breath, and all hopes from futurity are loſt. The fever has left me, but nothing of me remains but ſkin and bone. My ſon, (Kaum Bukſh,) though gone towards Beejapore, is ſtill near; and thou, my ſon, art yet nearer. The worthy of eſteem, Shaw Aulum, is far diſtant; and my grandſon, (Azeem Ooſhaun,) by the orders of God, is arrived near Hindoſtan. The camp and followers, helpleſs and alarmed, are, like myſelf, full of affliction, reſtleſs as the quickſilver. Separated from their lord, they know not if they have a maſter or not.

I brought nothing into this world, and, except the infirmities of man, carry nothing out. I have a dread for my ſalvation, and with what torments I may be puniſhed. Though I have ſtrong reliance on the mercies and bounty of God, yet, regarding my actions, fear will not quit me; but, when I am gone, reflection will not remain. Come then what may, I have launched my veſſel to the waves. Though Providence will protect the camp, yet, regarding appearances, the endeavours of my ſons are indiſpenſably incumbent. Give my laſt prayers to my grandſon, (Bedar Bukht,) whom I cannot ſee, but the deſire affects me. The Begum (his daughter) appears afflicted; but God is the only judge of hearts. The fooliſh thoughts of women produce nothing but diſappointment. Farewell! farewell! farewell!

To the Prince Kaum Buksh.

MY ſon, neareſt to my heart. Though in the height of my power, and by God's permiſſion, I gave you advice, and took with you the greateſt pains, yet, as it was not the divine will, you did not attend with the ears of compliance. Now I depart a ſtranger, and lament my own inſignificance, what does it profit me? I carry with me the fruits of my ſins and imperfections. Surprizing Providence! I came here alone, and alone I depart. The leader of this caravan hath deſerted me. The fever, which troubled me for twelve days, has left me. Wherever I look, I ſee nothing but the Divinity. My fears for the camp and followers are great; but, alas! I know not myſelf. My back is bent with weakneſs, and my feet have loſt the powers of motion.

7   The

dispatched the prince Azim Shaw towards Malwa, and Kaum Bukſh to his government of Beejapore. His reaſon for this proceeding was, that no feuds might ariſe upon his death, in an enemy's country, between his ſons, to endanger the repoſe of his ſubjects. Had the two princes remained together in the camp, ſuch would have been the caſe, as occurred afterwards on the death of Shaw Aulum, whoſe four ſons were together in the camp, when, though not in an enemy's country, the families, fortunes and honour of a world became plunged in the depth of ruin.

Azim Shaw, though knowing the dangerous illneſs of his father, dared not diſobey the orders of march. He departed from the camp, but his motions were ſlow and cautious; nor did the emperor preſs him to expedition, after the three firſt marches. He

---

The breath which roſe, is gone, and left not even hope behind it. I have committed numerous crimes, and know not with what puniſhments I may be ſeized. Though the Protector of mankind will guard the camp, yet care is incumbent alſo on the faithful, and my ſons. When I was alive, no care was taken; and now I am gone the conſequence may be gueſſed. The guardianſhip of a people is the truſt by God committed to my ſons. Azim Shaw is near. Be cautious that none of the faithful are ſlain, or their miſeries fall upon my head. I reſign you, your mother and ſon, to God, as I myſelf am going. The agonies of death come upon me faſt. Bahadur Shaw is ſtill where he was, and his ſon is arrived near Hindoſtan. Bedar Bukht is in Guzarat. Hyaut al Niſſa, who has beheld no afflictions of time till now, is full of ſorrows. Regard the Begum as without concern. Odiporee, your mother, was a partner in my illneſs, and wiſhes to accompany me in death; but every thing has its appointed time.

The domeſtics and courtiers, however deceitful, yet muſt not be ill-treated. It is neceſſary to gain your views by gentleneſs and art. Extend your feet no lower than your ſkirt. The complaints of the unpaid troops are as before. Dara Shekkoh, though of much judgment and good underſtanding, ſettled large penſions on his people, but paid them ill, and they were ever diſcontented. I am going. Whatever good or evil I have done, it was for you. Take it not amiſs, nor remember what offences I have done to yourſelf; that account may not be demanded of me hereafter. No one has ſeen the departure of his own ſoul; but I ſee that mine is departing.

C

A.H. 1118.
A.C. 1707.
Feb. 21ft.

even faid to [1] Hummeed ad dien Khan, to whom he had committed the charge of his funeral rites, " Three days after my death, one " of my fons will arrive in camp, and fend my remains to Aurun- " gabad in a proper manner." On Friday the twenty-eighth of Zeekaud, his majefty performed his morning devotions in company with his attendants ; after which, as was frequently his cuftom, he exclaimed, " O that my death may happen on a Friday, for "·bleffed is he who dieth on that day !" Soon after, he had occa- fion to retire. Upon his return towards his bed, he had begun the [2] tiummum, as was always his cuftom till water for the [3] wuzzoo could be brought, and had made one fprinkling, when fuddenly his moft pure fpirit fled from the narrownefs of corporeal confine- ment, to the boundlefs expanfion of the Moft High. We are from God, and to God we muft return. His hands remained clafped, and in motion, for fome time after he had ceafed to breathe. How can I exprefs my own feelings ? This much I know, that the kindnefs, favour and diftinction, for fifty years, of that atom- cherifhing fun to me, his humble flave, his great actions, his glory, his piety, his perfeverance in virtue from youth to age, the revolu- tions of his reign, and all the wonderful events of time, rufhed upon my memory at once in a fea of grief, and overwhelmed my heart, fo that I forgot myfelf, and knew not what paffed around me.

Azim Shaw, being informed of the event by his agents, and the nobles who affected to embrace his intereft, arrived on the third

[1] Anglicè, Aider of the faith.
[2] A purification by fprinkling of duft over the body, ordered by Mahummud for the convenience of his followers inhabiting the dry deferts of Arabia, where water is too valuable for the poor to ufe on flight occafions.
[3] Ditto with water.

4   of

of [1] Zeehudge at the camp at Ahmednuggur. He omitted no shew of affection and respect to his deceased father, but, like the orphans of those in humble life, shed many tears.

Many of the chief imperial servants, as [2] Muttullub Khan, [3] Khoddabundeh Khan, [4] Terbeut Khan, and others, had a real attachment to Azim Shaw. Some neither loved or hated him; and a few, though they disliked, yet, from inability to oppose, prudently submitted to his authority. Three Mogul chiefs only delayed to come in to offer their allegiance, [5] Feeroze Jung, his son Cheen Koollich Khan, and [6] Mahummud Ameen Khan.

On the tenth of Zeehuge, 1118, Azim Shaw ascended the A.C. 1707. throne of empire amidst the usual rejoicings, and conferred favours on the nobility according to their stations, but on few in a manner affording satisfaction. Here I must be permitted to mention one or two instances of the wonderful accomplishment of the decrees of Providence. While he was only a prince, most of the nobility were attached to Azim Shaw, and regarded him as possessing every approved quality for empire; but almost immediately after his accession to the throne, the general opinion was altered, from his own conduct. He slighted the principal nobility, and betrayed great parsimony to the army, acting as if he had no occasion for their services. This proceeded from a vain belief that none dared to oppose him, and that his elder brother, Shaw Aulum, relin-

---

[1] The twelfth month of the Arabian year.
[2] Anglicè, Object of the wish.
[3] Slave of God.
[4] Accomplished in manners and morals.
[5] Fortunate in war.
[6] Faithful in Mahummud.

quishing

quifhing to him fuch a vaft empire as Hindoftan, without a ftruggle, would fly for fafety to another clime.   At the fame time, he
openly declared his jealoufy of his own fon, Bedar Bukht, whofe
favour with the late emperor had difpleafed him.   He treated the
old nobility with contempt, and would fay publicly, that they were
not fit for his fervice.   He removed Terbeut Khan, a veteran and
loyal general, from his command of the artillery, in the moft in-
fulting manner, without any notice, and conferred that important
ftation on a young man of low rank among his creatures.   In
fhort, I cannot enumerate all the ill omens to the fortune of Azim
Shaw, which proved the will of Providence to have decreed heaven
beftowed empire to Shaw Aulum.   He who prideth in himfelf is
ruined.   When the will of God hath decreed an event, all things
aid the accomplifhment.

Mahummud Kaum Bukfh received intelligence of the emperor's
death, on his third day's march from Ahmednuggur, and was immediately deferted by Mahummud Ameen Khan, and all the Too-
raunee Moguls, though they had been purpofely appointed for his
protection, at this crifis, by Aulumgeer.   In addition to this mif-
fortune, ¹Zoolfeccar Khan, his bittereft enemy, who had once
confined him at the fiege of ²Iinjee, lay in his route with a confiderable army, fo that it was probable his perfon would be feized
by this nobleman, in order to obtain the favour of the new emperor.   Azim Shaw had difpatched orders to that effect; but Zoolfeccar Khan, either from policy or compaffion, did not obey them,
and Kaum Bukfh arrived in fafety at Beejapore, which he was al-

---

¹ Anglicè, Lord of the deftroying weapon.   This was the name of a fcymetar
belonging to Ali, fon-in-law to the prophet.
² A celebrated fortrefs in the Carnatic.

lowed to keep, as his brother, being eager to quit Dekkan, did not endeavour to remove him.

Azim Shaw now proceeded with the Imperial camp towards Agra, by regular stages, as if the principal of a caravan, and taking the route of Toomree, quitted the broad and easy road of Akberpore, on his left; proving, by this imprudent step, that, when destiny is unfavourable, man always doeth that which is wrong. The route of Toomree was hilly, full of woods, and, for many long spaces, void of water; so that, during two days march, great numbers of men, women, children, and animals, perished through fatigue and thirst. It was remarked by numbers, at the time, that this foreboded evil to the fortune of Azim Shaw; for he had rashly neglected the example of his father Aulumgeer, who, when marching against ¹ Dara Shekkoh, had chosen the route of Akberpore.

I must now return to the affairs of Bedar Bukht, whom it was my fortune to join. This prince, on the death of Aulumgeer, received orders from his father, Azim Shaw, to march immediately from Guzarat, and proceed towards Lahore, to prevent the advance of Shaw Aulum from Cabul. Bedar Bukht had the greatest and most sincere affection for his grandfather, who equally loved him; and on that account the father and son became jealous of each other. Upon receipt of the melancholy news, he was overwhelmed with real grief, which dwelt long upon his mind; for, when I saw him afterwards at Oojein, he would frequently weep at recollection of his loss. In obedience to the orders of his father, he departed from Guzarat without delay, at the head of only three thousand

---

¹ A most excellent and authentic account of this prince's adventures and misfortunes may be seen in Bernier's Travels, which are bound up in Churchill's and Lord Oxford's Collection of Voyages. Dow also details them; but I prefer Bernier's account, as more artless.

horse,

horfe, his own dependants, and carried with him about thirty lacks of rupees in treafure, property of his own, not prefuming to touch ¹ twenty lacks in the Imperial treafury, left it fhould raife fufpicions of his fidelity in the mind of his father. For the fame reafon, he made not any addition to his force, though he could with eafe have raifed a great army, and might have procured a ² corore of rupees from the bankers and renters, by way of loan, without oppreffion, as did ³ Moraud Bukfh, when he marched from this province againft Dara Shekkoh.

On the eve of his march, he difpatched a letter to me and feveral others on his route; but the couriers brought none to hand in due time, the public roads being guarded by officers, who had orders to fearch all meffengers, and infpect letters. As the prince expected me on the frontiers of Malwa, he was much difappointed on his arrival there, and repeatedly exclaimed, " What can have happened, " to prevent the coming of Eradut Khan?" My enemies, and feveral envious perfons, took occafion to defame me, faying, that I would never join him; for, knowing the jealoufy between him and his father, who was now emperor, I was gone to court his favour. In this manner did my enemies addrefs him, till he arrived near Oojein; when, not finding me there, in fpite of his regard and reliance upon me, fufpicion found room in his mind of my fidelity.

¹ Two hundred thoufand pounds.
² One million ditto.
³ Anglicè, Accomplifher of the wifh. Youngeft fon of the emperor Shaw Jehaun, and brother to Aulumgeer, who, having made ufe of him to attain the defeat of his elder brothers, confined him in the fortrefs of Gualiar, and afterwards had him put to death, on his being tried and condemned for murder, on the accufation of a dependant, whofe father he had executed for fome crime, when in power. Aulumgeer was obliged to difplace the firft judge before whom the caufe was brought, as he refufed to give fentence, faying, that a prince putting a man to death in the exercife of his authority, for a crime, ought not to be accounted murder.

At

At length, on the firſt of ¹Mohirrim, the prince's letters were A.H. 1119, A.C. 1707. brought me altogether, and immediately after, having loaded a ſmall tent and ſome neceſſaries on two trained camels, I departed from Mandou, leaving the fortreſs in charge of my dear relation and friend, Meer Sunjir.

The prince had been for ſome time encamped near Oojein, waiting for the lucky day to make his entry into that city, ſo that by chance I reached the camp at the inſtant of good fortune. He was moving in his ²nallekee towards the town, when he perceived me at a diſtance, and ſaid to his attendants, "Is not that Eradut "Khan that I ſee?." And was ſcarcely anſwered, when I came up. He ſtopped his train, and opening wide his arms, cried, "Come, "come my friend! in expectation of whom my eyes have been "ſtretched, even to dimneſs." I kiſſed his feet, and preſented my offering. He preſſed my head to his boſom, and taking off his ³neem-aſteen, put it on my ſhoulders. His firſt words were lamentations mingled with tears, for the deceaſed emperor his grandfather, for whom he knew the ſincerity of my grief. He then ordered me to mount my horſe, and ride near him; and, as we proceeded to the city, related all that had happened to himſelf, and his anxiety at not meeting me on the borders of the province. When I had ſatisfied him for my delay, he commanded thoſe who had ſpoken againſt me to quit his preſence, with much diſpleaſure, and refuſed to admit them again for many days.

¹ The firſt month of the Arabian year.

² A canopied litter peculiar to the princes, and allowed now and then to ſome few great officers of ſtate. It is generally of rich materials, and often entirely of ſilver. It is carried on the ſhoulders of twelve or ſixteen bearers, on three poles, one on each ſide, like our ſedans, and the third running under the middle of the machine.

³ An upper robe with half-ſleeves, commonly made of gold or ſilver tiſſue. For a prince, or perſon of high rank, to confer any part of his own dreſs on an inferior, is accounted a very great honour to the receiver.

Bedar

Bedar Bukht did not remain in the palace of Oojein; but, after viewing the city, pitched his camp on the bank of the river, at about a cofs diftant. Here he was attended by [1] Abdoollah Khan, the foubadar of Malwa, and continued one month and twenty days, expecting the arrival of his father, when that rafh prince wrote him the following firmaun:

" Why have you not haftened on, nor funk the boats in the
" [2] Suttulludge, to prevent the approach of the enemy? Though
" he dare not face me, yet you have been guilty of high neglect."

Soon after my arrival in camp, the prince fent a [3] Nifhaun, with the following words in his own hand, to my dear fon [4] Huddaiut Oollah Khan, then Fojedaur of a diftrict of about two days journey from Oojein.

" Your father, one of my moft efteemed dependants, attends
" the ftirrup. I am furprized that you have not as yet come to the
" prefence."

My fon, in reply, wrote to the prince, that he fhould fhortly feek the honour of an audience; but privately to me, defiring that I would reprefent to his highnefs, what refpect would not permit him to mention himfelf. This was, that though I had no force under me, yet my attendance and advice might be of ufe; but that he, unlefs at the head of troops, could do no fervice; that he had then with him two thoufand veteran foldiers, all his followers for twenty years, who would accompany him without the limits of his

---

[1] Slave of God.
[2] One of the five great rivers between Cabul and Lahore.
[3] The letters of the emperor are ftyled firmauns, thofe of princes, nifhauns.
[4] Directed by God.

government.

government. Of thefe he had fent a return to the prince, whom he would immediately attend, on the advance of a month's pay to enable him to march; but without that they muft be excufed.

His highnefs, in anfwer to this meffage, faid to me, "To give "Huddaiut Oollah this fum, or much greater, I would not hefi- "tate; but, alas! fhould I call in fuch a force, as your attachment "to me has been reprefented to my father in a fufpicious view by "interefted perfons, he would inftantly, on the junction of your "fon's troops, be convinced of my difloyalty, and turn his arms "from Shaw Aulum againft me. Write this to your fon." I did fo; and he declined coming to the camp, writing to me the following words: "I refign you to the protection of a gracious "God, fince I am prevented by my ill-fortune from paying my "duty in perfon. I wifh you could leave the party with which "you are engaged, as I fee deftiny will to it prove unfavorable." God be praifed, that from his prudent caution, my dear fon remained fecure from the enfuing troubles.

Bedar Bukht, agreeable to the orders of his father, moved towards Agra, and was joined from the prefence by Zoolfeccar Khan, Ram Sing Harrah, zemindar of [1] Koteh, and Dulput [2] Bonedela, alfo Amaun Oolla Khan, who were fent by Azim Shaw,

---

[1] A principal zemindary in Malwa, now much circumfcribed by the Mharattas, who allow the raja, a defcendant of Ram Sing's, but a very fmall proportion of his lands.

[2] The Bonedela tribe of Rajapootes are the poffeffors of Bonedelcund, an extenfive tract, lying partly in the Agra, and partly in the province of Allahabad. Their proper chief, the raja of Oorcha, defcended from Ber Sing Deo, the founder of the family importance, poffeffes but little territory, far the greateft part having been wrefted from his houfe by Chutterfaul, one of a younger branch of the Bonedelas, whofe defcendants now hold his eftates jointly with the Mharattas, who have a third part of the lands, and produce of the diamond mines of Pirna.

D

as much to guard the prince's motions as to affift him.   [1] Meerza Raja Jey Sing, [2] Khan Aulum a Dekkan chief, with his brother [3] Munnower Khan, and other officers, alfo joined from the prefence, with about fix thoufand horfe.

The prince [4] Mahummud Azeem Ooſhawn, who had, by Aulumgeer's orders, left his government of Bengal to proceed to the prefence, had reached the vicinity of Agra, when he heard of the emperor's deceafe; upon which he marched to fecure that city for his father, Shaw Aulum. [5] Mukhtar Khan, the foubadar, who was attached to Azim Shaw, and father-in-law to Bedar Bukht, hoping to impede his progrefs, funk all the boats in the Jumna, and placed guards at the neareft fords. But, alas! what power had fuch a vaffal to face the fon of his decreed fovereign? The prince moved higher up, and having croffed the river, took him prifoner; but regarding his former fervices, and thofe of his

[1] Zemindar of a confiderable territory in the province of Ajmere, named Ambeer; but fince this prince's founding a new city called Jeypore, the rajaſhip has alfo taken that name. Jeypore is reckoned the moft regular built city in Hindoftan; and Europeans, who have feen it, fpeak highly of its magnificence. Jey Sing was a great encourager of fcience, and built feveral obfervatories for aftronomical ftudies. He alfo erected a caravanferai and market in every province of Hindoftan, for the convenience of travellers, at his own expence. The prefent raja of Jeypore, his grand-nephew, poffeffes the city, but not much territory, part of which has been feized by vaffals of his family, and part by the Mharattas and Mogul chiefs, to both of whom he is tributary. Jeypore is the great mart for horfes from Perfia and the northern provinces of Hindoftan; and the old citadel of Ambeer, clofe to it, is faid to contain vaft wealth laid up by Jey Sing. This will probably one day fall into the hands of the Mharattas, if they are not foon diverted from their operations in this part of India, by troubles in Dekkan, that ſhall furniſh them employment nearer home.

[2] Anglicè, Lord of the world.

[3] Enlightened lord

[4] Anglicè, Of high dignity; fecond fon of Shaw Aulum, the eldeft furviving fon of Aulumgeer.

[5] Anglicè, Powerful lord.

family,

family, did not offer him perfonal injuries. It had as yet been the ufage of the princes of this illuftrious houfe, though a nobleman according to his connections with one of them, appeared againft another in the field, that the victor did not put him to death, or difgrace him. On the contrary, the fidelity and valour difplayed by him, in the caufe of a defeated rival, were fure recommendations to the conqueror's favour. The princes knew that the ftability of power and regulation of empire refted on the fupport of an experienced nobility, and they would frequently obferve, " that their " enmity was not to the throne; for whenever a prince became " fixed upon it, they were faithful fubjects. If then we deftroy " them, through whom can we adminifter the government." By this wife policy of the Imperial family, the rules and order of the extenfive empire of Hindoftan remained uninjured by the quarrels of the princes.—But to return to my fubject.

When Mahummud Bedar Bukht approached the banks of the [1] Chumbul, and Azim Shaw arrived near [2] Gualiar, Azeem Oofhawn detached a confiderable body from Agra, under [3] Motufhum Khan, to guard the fords. Bedar Bukht was fond of enterprize, jealous of his honour, and of high mind tempered with prudence. A rivalfhip for glory had always fubfifted between him and his father, Azim Shaw, who was of rafh courage, and never looked beyond the prefent in his conduct. Like the [4] whifker-twifting vaunters

[1] A river in the province of Agra.

[2] One of the moft celebrated fortreffes of Hindoftan, an elegant plate of which, with the account of its capture by a detachment under colonel Popham, in 1780, has been given to the public by major Rennell; but another, on a larger fcale, with a more minute defcription of the place, is now preparing by the ingenious Mr. W. Hodges, well known for his drawings under Captain Cook, and for his views of places in India, taken by himfelf on the fpot.

[3] Dignified.

[4] The twift of the whifkers in India, and the outrageous cock of the hat in England, are alike characterriftic.

of

of Hindoſtan, if his ſon made any delay on his march, he would
jeſt and ſneer, attributing it to cowardice, and dread of the enemy.
On this account, Bedar Buhkt reſolved to croſs the Chumbul immediately, and attack the poſts of Motuſhum Khan; but this
proceeding was ſtrongly oppoſed by Zoolfeccar Khan, an experienced general of approved conduct; upon which a ſtrange contention took place, which is worthy of relation.

A number of low-minded perſons, vain and imprudent, ſuch as
are too frequently the favorites of princes, who thought themſelves
capable antagoniſts for the nobility of Azeem Oſhawn, regarding
this as a fit opportunity to ſhew their loyalty and attachment, interfered in the conduct of affairs. As Zoolfeccar Khan, in the
opinion of ſome, was ſuſpected of treachery, they ſeized this occa-
ſion to perſuade the prince that he correſponded with Shaw Aulum,
and wiſhed to delay engaging till his approach, in order to complete his deſigns of deſertion to his cauſe. God only knows the
heart, and perhaps it might have been ſo; but, in the eye of underſtanding, good policy alone ſeemed to influence his conduct in
this affair.

When he was informed that the prince had reſolved on croſſing
the river the next morning, he repeatedly repreſented, through the
proper officers, that ſuch a ſtep was by no means adviſeable at the
preſent criſis; but the prince refuſed to take his opinion. Upon
this, Zoolfeccar Khan went himſelf to his highneſs's tents, and
requeſted an audience, ſetting forth, that he had affairs of importance to communicate; but the prince would not admit him, and
ſent word, that nightly council was unlucky, therefore he muſt
wait till the morning. I had heard of Zoolfeccar Khan's advice
during the day, and of the prince's diſſent, but knew not what had
paſſed at night; for I made it a rule never to go to his councils,

                                                              unleſs

unlefs called upon; and his highnefs had never failed, till now, to fend for me. It happened, that I had been this day to vifit Zoolfeccar Khan, at his earneft requeft, but not a word on the affair in debate paffed between us. Some envious perfons, however, took this occafion to perfuade the prince, that I was a partner with the general; and, notwithftanding his conviction of my fidelity, his highnefs, in his prefent humour, believed them. Hence it is, that the ancients obferved, "We fhould never rely on the favour of "princes; for when their minds are difgufted, though without "caufe, a thoufand years of confidence may be deftroyed in one "inftant of fufpicion."

The day following, fuddenly, before morning prayer, the march of battle was founded, and the prince, completely armed, mounted the elephant which he always rode in the day of action. I was at my devotions, when I heard the drums; but dreffing myfelf in hafte and aftonifhment, I fpeeded to attend him. He had moved fome diftance from the tents before I came up. I found him, with an angry countenance, and contemptuous exclamation, uttering reproachful terms of Zoolfeccar Khan, as deceiver, traitor, falfe wretch, and the like, to fome fervile attendants round his elephant; but, on perceiving me, he became filent, and looked more difpleafed. According to cuftom, I alighted from my horfe to make my obeifance, of which he took no notice, nor fpoke, nor fmiled upon me as he was wont to do, but turned his head another way. Though much hurt at this flight, I took my ftation as ufual on his right hand, clofe to the ear of his elephant, and ruminated on the change in his behaviour, while my enemies, who during the night had formed this ¹ telifm, were rejoicing all around at my diftrefs. Though his highnefs did not fpeak to them after my

¹ Charm, or talifman.

arrival,

arrival, yet I judged, by their exulting, and winking to one another, that fomewhat highly pleafing to them had happened.

Juft then, Zoolfeccar Khan fent an officer to requeft I would attend him; for he hoped that, at my defire, the prince would alter his intention of paffing the river. I informed his highnefs of the officer's coming, for I never vifited any of the nobility without permiffion. Upon this, he angrily exclaimed, " Go! ' Your " quiver alfo hangs at his belt! " I then defired the officer to return, and tell what he had heard, as I could not go; but the prince, with a furious afpect, cried out, " Be gone! Why don't " you go to your friend? " At beholding this, a giddinefs feized my brain, and I became diftracted; for I never expected fuch words from him, whofe favour I thought fincere, and prided my-felf on deferving, by my fidelity. I became raging, rafh, and im-petuous, and faid, " What bufinefs can I, the humbleft of the " humble, have with nobles of Zoolfeccar's exalted rank? He " was the firft general of your grandfather; but your father has " now detached him under your command, and certainly the " power is at prefent in your hands, to treat him as you pleafe." His highnefs, upon this, more angrily than ever, exclaimed, " Surely the emperor hath not made you my tutor! " What fhall I fay? Heaven and earth feemed to fall at once upon my fhoulders, and I wifhed to die that inftant; but thefe words invo-luntarily flipped from my tongue: " What is my ability, to be-" come tutor to a prince like your highnefs? Yet, fhould the truft " be offered me, I would rather fly from fociety with a fhorn head, " than accept it." To this he made no reply, and I quitted his perfon without ceremony.

' An idiomatical expreffion, fignifying that he was attached to his party.

I had

I had not gone far, when the generous, forbearing, patient and benevolent prince, cherisher of his friends, sent to me the [1]daroga of his khowaus, to say, as from himself, " What troublesome " dreams hath my friend seen, to disorder his imagination, and " make him rave? Know you not, that spies have prejudiced my " father against you, as my adviser? Therefore, as much con- " tention passed last night, between me and Zoolfeccar Khan, and " I have just now insulted that deceitful traitor, I spoke angrily to " you also, to remove suspicion of my treatment of him proceeding " from your counsel, not supposing you could misapprehend me." Upon this, I stopped till the prince came up, when he called me to him, and smiling, whispered in my ear, " I have beheld your " deep penetration." I replied, " I did not expect such expressions " from your highness." He answered, " I also wished to try " your patience, my friend, who pretend to so much prudence, " with such heat and passion." Having said this, he took from his neck a large cornelian of [2]Yemmun, on which were engraved some prayers in a beautiful character, and giving it to me, said aloud, " Admire this graving!" at the same time nodding that I should keep it; but I returned it, signifying privately, that the gift was improper before so many envious witnesses. At length, my late exulting and mean-spirited enemies, seeing me again in favour, retired to a distance, and left me to converse with his high- ness; who then said, " Surely you must have forgotten what my " father wrote to me, concerning you, three days since, and my " answer to his majesty!" That affair I will relate.

The prince had three days before received a firmaun under his father's own hand, and I went with him to meet it, agreeable to custom. About midnight, he sent for me again, and carried me

[1] Overseer of domestic attendants.   [2] Arabia Felix.

into the sleeping apartment of his ¹mahal, where he had been
sitting with the mother of ²Bedar Dil, who retired as I came in, to
another chamber.   He gave me the firmaun, and desired me to read
it.   In it was written, in Azim Shaw's own hand, the following
sentence: " You are day and night consulting with Eradut Khan;
" I wish to know for what purpose!"   When I had returned the
paper, his highness asked what was fit to write in answer.

I replied, " I am your servant.   Dismiss me for the present,
" and when my duty is requisite, I will instantly return."   He
exclaimed,   " You must not leave me ; but some answer must be
" written.   I will attempt one;   but you must also compose
" another, and we will send that we both approve."   He then gave
me pen, ink and paper, from his standish, and seated me at a lamp.
He wrote, and I wrote.   When we had finished, it appeared, on
comparison, that we had both written the same, almost without
the difference of a word, as follows :

" It must be remembered in the sacred mind, that your majesty,
" in passing through Malwa to the presence of the Shadow of
" God, said to your slave, *Eradut Khan is our household servant,*
" *truly loyal, wise and experienced.   I give him to you, that, when*
" *important affairs shall come in agitation, you may consult with him.*
" Health to your majesty !   What crisis of affairs can be more im-
" portant than the present ?   According to the orders founded in
" benevolence, I do consult with him daily, on all affairs public
" and private.   I know not what suspicions those admitted to the
" presence may have formed of this faithful servant, but, were
" they communicated to me, I could remove them to the satisfac-
" tion of your majesty."

¹ The ladies apartments.   ² His son; Anglicè, Vigilant mind.   ³ The
emperor Aulumgeer.

The

The prince applauded me much, and faid, " with this able
" judgement and the fimilarity of our difpofitions, how can I
" avoid giving you my efteem ? " But to be fincere in this affair,
juftice was on the fide of Azim Shaw; for Bedar Bukht was rival
to his father, and waited opportunity to dethrone him. As for
me, I was never in the fervice of Azim Shaw, nor had ever made
him profeffions of duty, being wholly devoted to his fon.

Being alone with him one night, he fuddenly threw his arms
about my neck, and holding down his head upon my breaft, faid,
" If a fovereign and parent feeks the life of a fon, and that fon is
" truly informed of his intention, how fhould he act in felf-
" defence ? Have you a precedent for it ? "

I replied, " Such a queftion is unneceffary. The behaviour of
" your ¹ grandfather to his father is a fufficient precedent ; and
" fovereigns are forced to expedients which are not juftifiable in
" other men."

Converfation of this fort often paffed between us ; and one
evening he afked me, how he might gain an opportunity of feizing
his father. I replied, " An opportunity will offer thus : When
" he has gained the victory over Shaw Aulum, you will be the
" firft to congratulate him. The troops will then be feparated
" here and there in fearch of plunder, or looking after the dead
" and wounded ; and, as the tents will not be ready, your father
" will be only under a ² fhaumianeh, furrounded by a few ³ kanauts.

¹ Alluding to Aulumgeer's dethronement of Shaw Jehaun.
² A canopy of cotton cloth.
³ Walls of cotton cloth, which are always pitched round the tents of all who can
afford them. The principal chiefs have them, enclofing ground of a great extent
round theirs. They have a very fplendid appearance. Bernier gives a good defcription of a Mogul camp, to which the curious may refer.

E   " You

" You will be admitted to audience, attended by such of your fol-
" lowers as may have deserved notice in the action by their gallant
" conduct; and, at such a time, they will be allowed their arms.
" It is probable your father will not have many persons with him
" between the kanauts. Then is your time."   The prince eagerly
exclaimed, " You have spoken well! Dare you, at such a time,
" strike the blow?"

I replied, that though the act was easy, yet a sacred oath rested
upon our family never to shed the blood of a prince unless by
chance in battle, if engaged in the cause of a rival, when it would
be excusable.   I then said, " Your other opportunity will be thus:
" should the enemy fly, an army will be sent in pursuit, and pro-
" bably under your command, while your father, setting his mind
" at ease, will be employed, without suspicion, in pleasure and
" rejoicing. You may return suddenly upon him, and gain your
" wishes.   Should this opportunity not occur, as you are his eldest
" son and have seen much service, he will certainly appoint you to
" the government of Dekkan.   You will have then a powerful
" army at your disposal.   As your father's behaviour is disgustful
" to the people, and many of the courtiers dislike him, they will
" aid your pretensions. Use open force, and try for whom God
" will decide."

Bedar Bukht, having crossed the Chumbul at an unobserved
ford, the troops of Azeem Ooshaun, who were stationed on the
banks of the river in another quarter, left their artillery in the
various posts, and fled to Agra, happy to save their lives. Zoolfeccar, who had advised the prince to remain on the other side,
seeing he had crossed, now came up reluctantly, and congratulated
him on the success of his march. This submission pleasing his
highness, he resolved on the morrow to honour him with a visit,

7   in

in order to atone for his late behaviour. Zoolfeccar Khan, hearing of his intention, fent a meffage to me, defiring that I would perfuade him to lay it afide, as his highnefs's vifit would occafion various reports, and the caufe be inferted in the intelligence of the fpies, with remarks that would injure the prince and himfelf in the opinion of Azim Shaw.

I was preparing to execute the commiffion; but before I could leave my tent, Zoolfeccar Khan paffed by, having refolved to go himfelf to the prince. Begging pardon for his boldnefs, he pre-fented a ¹garland of flowers to his highnefs, who, foftened with his humility, fhewed him more favour than was confiftent with his own dignity. It was a rule of Aulumgeer's, never to fhew fuch condefcenfion to the nobility, as to make them think themfelves too neceffary to him, but he conducted himfelf fo as to be held in refpectful veneration by thofe even neareft his perfon. Certain it is, that too much humility in a fovereign lofes him the object for which it is affumed. The prince, having honoured him with the robe he had on, and a rich ²firpeach of jewels, difmiffed him with numerous profeffions of kindnefs.

Zoolfeccar Khan the fame evening made another vifit, when I only was fitting with the prince, and thus began to offer his advice: " Since your highnefs has croffed the river, as the prince Azeem " Ooſhaun is near, it is proper to march towards him immediately, " left your father ſhould conceive evil fufpicions, or the army

---

¹ Garlands made of the chumbeely, a fort of double jafmine, are always introduced with the betel at entertainments, and prefented to the guefts; alfo taffels of the fame for the turban, and fometimes leaves of gold and filver foils, are interwoven with the flowers.

² The firpeach is a jewel for the turban. A kulghee, or egret, is generally worn with it.

" fuppofe

" suppose that you fear to engage him." The prince did not
answer him, but nodding to me, said, " Have you heard what he
" observed ?" I replied, " Yes ; and he is an experienced general
" and faithful servant ; yet there are some points to be considered.
" Though engaging Azeem Ooshaun is no hazardous enterprize,
" yet he is also a prince ; and if, now your highness has crossed
" the river to meet him, he does not march this way, the reproach
" of delay will rest on him.   Let us consider also who is nearest to
" us, Azim Shaw, or Shaw Aulum.   If the former, let us march :
" yet Azeem Ooshaun, if defeated, has the city of Agra for a re-
" fuge, to reduce which must require some days.   His father may
" also arrive with his vast army, said to be an hundred thousand
" horse, and he has already with him thirty thousand.   If Zool-
" feccar Khan judges he can, without the aid of your father,
" engage these two armies, and a prince of Shaw Aulum's expe-
" rience and valour, what can we dread ? Let us march." Zoolfeccar Khan, in reply to this, only said, as was his manner when
pleased, " Good ! good ! good ! He hath spoken well."

Some days after this, Azim Shaw approaching near, Bedar Bukht
moved a cofs in front, the spot he was upon being chosen for his
father's tents ; and the morning of his arrival, went two cofs from
the camp to meet him.   Azim Shaw loved him as a son, though,
from the attention shewn him by Aulumgeer, he had regarded him
as a rival.   When he now beheld him, after long absence, paternal
fondness for the instant overcame his jealousy, and he received him
with strong marks of affection, conferring upon him a princely
khelaut, with the ' chaurkub, a sword set with jewels, elephants
and horses.   The prince, after the interview, asked me if I would
not pay my respects to his father : to which I replied, that I did

' An upper robe, never conferred but on princes of the royal family, the vizier of
the empire, and Ameer al Amra.

5   not

not wifh it, having no defire to engage his notice, or embrace his fervice; but, upon his obferving that my declining it would occafion much fufpicion, I confented, and was introduced. Azim Shaw, upon feeing me, faid, " Are you alfo come ?" I replied, " Yes, " but without orders. I left my ftation, though far diftant from " the route of your majefty. Who elfe has done fo ?" He conferred the ufual khelaut upon me, and gave orders for my being employed.

Empire having been decreed to Shaw Aulum, from the agency of deftiny, fuch vanity took poffeffion of the mind of Azim Shaw, that he was convinced his brother, though fupported by the myriads of ' Toor and Sullum, durft not meet him in the field. Hence, thofe who brought intelligence of his approach he would abufe as fools and cowards, fo that no one cared to fpeak the truth; as was formerly the cafe with the emperor ' Humaioon, during the rebellion of the Afghan Shere Shaw. Even his chief officers feared to difclofe intelligence, fo that he was ignorant of the fuccefsful progrefs of his rival.

At length Shaw Aulum having reached ' Muttra, fent by a celebrated dirvefh the following meffuage to Azim Shaw. " By the " divine aufpices, we inherit from our anceftors an extenfive " empire, comprehending many kingdoms. It will be juft and " glorious not to draw the fword againft each other, nor confent

---

1. Vaft armies, mentioned in the Koraun.
2. Father of Akber. See his reign in Dow's Hiftory.
3. A city about eighteen cofs N. of Agra, much venerated by the Hindoos, it being the birth-place of their god Kifhen. There were formerly very rich temples in it; but one, more celebrated than the reft, and erected by Ber Sing, deo raja of Oorcha, coft thirty-fix lacks of rupees. It was razed by Aulumgeer, who built a mofque on the fite with the materials. Muttra, however, has ftill many temples, which are vifited by pilgrims from all parts of India.

" to

" to fhed the blood of the faithful. Let us equally divide the
" empire between us. Though I am the elder, I will leave the
" choice in your power." Azim Shaw, vain-glorious and haughty,
replied, that he would anfwer his brother on the morrow in the
field, and upon this, the meffenger departed. Azim Shaw marched
the next morning, and encamped between Iajoo and Agra, on a
barren plain void of water, fo that the army was much diftreffed.
Intelligence arrived during this day, that Shaw Aulum was
encamped feven cofs diftant, and intended moving on the morrow,
but to what quarter was not known.

I have already mentioned, that my defign is not to write the
hiftory of kings, but of myfelf, and what I have feen. Accordingly, of the battle between the brothers, I fhall only relate fuch
circumftances as I was an eye-witnefs of.

Sunday, the 18th of Ru-bee al awul, A. H. 1119. A. C. 1707. The morning dawned; but what a dawn! Darting fire, and tinged with blood; of whofe horrors the laft day can only prove an imitation. Call it not morning; it was the day of judgment! Call it not dawn; it was the evening of death! Call it not day, but the gloomy eve of the woes of time!

Mahummud Bedar Bukht, who commanded the advanced corps
of the army, having given the neceffary orders, began his march.
He was mounted upon his favorite elephant, and his moft valued
attendants were near his perfon. Zoolfeccar Khan with the two
Raujepoet chiefs, Ram Sing and Dulput Roy, alfo Amaun Oollah
Khan, followed them, inclined fomewhat to the left of the prince.
The main body of the army marched next, in the center of which
rode Azim Shaw, furrounded by his courtiers and a numerous
band of Mogul, Afghan and Hindoftanee ¹munfubdaurs, of

¹ Anglicè, Holding rank. Perfons of family, but without titles of nobility.

approved

approved valour. We had not as yet learned the pofition of the enemy, or what was the defign of Shaw Aulum.

Mahummud Bedar Bukht had reached a village, near which was a ftream of clear water; and fome wells were alfo round about it. The troops at this time were much feparated, and every chief, inattentive to order, moved as he chofe. Seeing which, I reprefented to the prince, that the main body was far behind; that the country in his front was deftitute of water for fome miles, and the day promifed to be diftreffingly hot. Without order, without intelligence of the enemy's motions, where would he haften? I remarked the fcattered march of his followers; Zoolfeccar Khan obliqued fo far to the left as fcarcely to be vifible, and other chiefs equally diftant in every quarter. I obferved, that, if he halted here till fome news arrived of the enemy, there was fufficient water to refrefh the troops, the artillery would come up, the emperor have time to join, and order be reftored in the line; alfo that, fhould the enemy advance upon him, he would have the advantage of good ground and plenty of water. He replied, " Your advice is juft. Go, and " inform my father I fhall follow it."

It happened alfo, that Shaw Aulum had no advice of the route of our army; and, as there was but little water where he was encamped, he had this morning difpatched his main body under [1] Monauim Khan, while he, with his fons and perfonal attendants, hunted along the bank of the Jumna. His [2] peefhkhaneh, with the ufual efcort under [3] Rooftum-dil Khan, was coming on in front of the army, in the fame route as our line.

[1] Anglicè, Fortunate. He was chief minifter to Shaw Aulum.

[2] Anglicè, Advanced houfe. The Hindoftanee chiefs have always two fets of tents, &c. one of which is always difpatched, in front of the army, to the next ground of encampment, and pitched for their reception.

[3] Anglicè, Of heart like Rooftum, the celebrated champion of Firdofi's Shaw-nammeh, or Hiftory of Perfian Kings.

Upon

Upon the delivery of my meffage to Azim Shaw, he replied,
" It is very well. Go, and inform my fon I am coming up."   I
returned to the promifed place of halt; but what did I behold!
The prince had marched on, and left the village unguarded.   I
fpeeded after him, and, upon gaining the line, faw a joyful fcene
of congratulation on victory. When the prince faw me, he eagerly
exclaimed, " I congratulate you on victory!"   I replied, " How
" comes victory, without a battle ?"   Upon which his highnefs,
turning to a courier, faid, " Tell Eradut Khan what you have feen."
This foolifh wretch then affirmed, that he had feen the ' Sewarree
elephant of Shaw Aulum, without a rider, and with but few attendants, running off towards Agra.   The prince then faid, that
our left wing had defeated the enemy, and taken all their baggage.
The caufe of this imaginary victory was thus : The advanced
baggage of Shaw Aulum falling in with our left wing, was attacked, and, the efcort being fmall, foon taken.   The elephant feen
running away, belonged to Rooftum-dil Khan, who commanded
the efcort.

The prince, however, now ordered me to go and inform his
father of the victory, fuppofing that my being the bearer of good
news would give me favour in his mind. I declined going, and
obferved, that I could not carry intelligence fo very ridiculous and
groundlefs ; upon which the prince was angry, and exclaimed,
" What do you mean ?"   I replied, " Let us reafon on the fub-
" ject. Is not Shaw Aulum the fon of Aulumgeer, and claimant
" of the throne ? Has he not advanced from Cabul to Agra, with
" four fons, valiant like himfelf, and a great army ? Can then any
" perfon of judgment even fuppofe, that he fhould bafely fly
" without a battle, or even having feen his enemy ? What dread

---

' That on which he ufually rode.

" can

" can have feized him, who was a valiant leader in the wars of
" Dekkan, againft ¹ Samba, ² Sunta, and ³ Dhunna? Accidents
" will happen to the baggage of armies, and this boafted victory
" is no more. Your troops have plundered his advanced tents;
" but woe to thofe who have been thus employed! If important
" fervice fhould now offer, they will be ufelefs, confufed as they
" are, and encumbered with fpoil." To thefe remarks the prince
angrily exclaimed, " You are always apprehenfive, and foreboding
" ill!" He then ordered Cafim, the ⁴ darogah of his divan, to
carry the intelligence of victory to Azim Shaw.

Scarce half an hour after this had elapfed, when a great duft
arofe upon our right. Upon this, I faid to the prince, " Behold
" the confequence of our victory, and the flight of Shaw Aulum!
" Yon cloud precedes at leaft fifty thoufand horfe." Juft as I
had concluded, another duft arofe, which certified a fecond body
of troops approaching. I defired his highnefs to prepare for action,
while yet the enemy was at fome diftance. He then faid, " Will
" you now go, and inform my father of the enemy's approach?"
To this I replied, " Though I wifh not to quit your highnefs's
" perfon, yet, as I am ordered, I muft obey;" and, having faid
this, I rode off with fpeed towards Azim Shaw. On my way, I
beheld ftrange diforder. Amaun Oollah Khan, a reputed good
officer, who acted as ⁵ herauwul to the prince ⁶ Wallajah, I met
with only two or three hundred ftraggling horfe. Azim Shaw was

---

¹ Son to the celebrated Mharatta chief Sewajee, whom he fucceeded; but was taken
prifoner, and put to death by Aulumgeer.
² Another fon of Sewajee.
³ A famous Mharatta chief.
⁴ Superintendant of the hall of audience.
⁵ Leader of the advanced corps.
⁶ Anglicè, Of high rank. He was younger fon to Azim Shaw.

a cofs

a cofs and a half farther in the rear, and his troops become fepe-
rated into three divifions, fo that I could not eafily diftinguifh the
royal poft; for the train of artillery had been left in Dekkan, and
the ftandard elephants were out of their ftations, fo that there was
nothing to mark the emperor from a diftance. When Terbeut
Khan was removed from the command of the artillery, and his
fucceffor applied for orders concerning it to Azim Shaw, he was
much enraged, and paffionately exclaimed, " Do men think that I
" will ufe cannon againft a 'breeder of cattle? I will not even
" draw the fword, but bruife his head with a ftaff."

At length I perceived the imperial ²umbrella, and haftened towards it. Some of the courtiers, who always firft received intelligence, that they might accommodate it to the humour of their
mafter, demanded my bufinefs; but, not liftening to fuch weak
flatterers, I rode on. When Azim Shaw faw me, he made a fignal
for me to advance; but, fuch was the crowd, I had fcarce ability
to pufh through it. At length, having come near to his ³travelling
throne, I alighted from my horfe, and faid, " The prince informs
" your majefty of the enemy's near approach." What fhall I fay?
Azim Shaw, ftarting as if ftung by a fcorpion, with furious looks,
eyes rolling, and, as was his cuftom when angry, pulling up his
fleeve, exclaimed, " Comes an enemy to me!" Being vexed at
his manner, I replied, " So it appears." He then called aloud for
his war elephant, and, in a frantic manner whirling a ⁴crooked

¹ Alluding to the bullocks ufed for the draft of the artillery, univerfal in Hindoftan.
² The umbrella is one of the imperial enfigns; and, when the etiquette of the court
was kept up, no fubject dared to carry one.
³ A feat, or rather fmall couch, fixed on three poles, like the nallekee defcribed in a
former note.
⁴ A fhort crooked ftaff, about three feet in length, not unlike a crofier, ufed by
fakeers to lean on when they fit, and often by perfons of rank as an emblem of humility, and having declared themfelves difciples to fome holy man.

staff,

ſtaff, ſtood upright in his throne, and tauntingly ſaid, " Be not
" alarmed! I am coming up to my ſon." Hurt at this inſult to
the ſpirit of my prince, I ſaid, " His highneſs is ſon to yourſelf,
" aſylum of a world, and knoweth not fear. He only repreſents
" the enemy's approach, that your majeſty may advance with the
" troops, and take the poſt uſual for the emperor in the day of
" battle."

Having ſaid this, I rode off to rejoin Bedar Bukht; but ſuch
crowds ſurrounded me to aſk for news, that I could not diſengage
myſelf till within a rocket's flight of the prince. Juſt as I had
reached him, the enemy began to cannonade, and a ball ſtruck the
breaſt of an attendant cloſe to his perſon.

As I had not been undreſſed for the laſt two nights, and was
exceedingly fatigued with hard riding, the ſun and wind being
burning hot, my ſtrength now failed me, and I fainted away. My
brother, ſeeing this, lifted me from my horſe, laid me on the
ground, and looſened my armour, but could get no water to revive
me. The prince, obſerving my diſtreſs, generouſly ſent me a ſmall
veſſel from his elephant, which gave me new life. I untied the
folds of my veſt, and poured ſome of the water on my breaſt, but
was ſtill too faint to riſe. By this time, Azim Shaw was come up;
but, contrary to the cuſtom of the emperors, whoſe ſtation is the
rear of the center, puſhed on towards Bedar Bukht, and his
attendants crowded after him without order. Ameer Khan paſſing
by, and ſeeing me on the ground, offered me a ſeat with him on
his elephant, as did others of my friends; but I refuſed them all.
At length my own elephant arriving, I mounted, and lay with my
breaſt bare upon three ſkins of water, which luckily for me were
in the ſeat, to prevent my fainting a ſecond time. The train elephants of Azim Shaw, thoſe of his women, of the treaſury, and

F 2   the

the jewel office, now pufhed between me and Bedar Bukht, fo that I was removed fome diftance from him.

The two bodies of the enemy had now approached, and halted within a ¹ rocket's flight of our line.   One of thefe was headed by the prince Azeem Oofhaun, the other by Monauim Khan, with whom were alfo the princes ² Moiz ad Dien Jehaundar Shaw and ³ Jehaun Shaw.   Our line was fo preffed upon on each flank, and in the rear, by baggage elephants, cattle and followers, as greatly to incommode the troops, and render them ufelefs.   Shaw Aulum's artillery played upon us inceffantly, and did great execution; and his fons advancing, fired fhowers of mufquetry, which fell like hail.   A line of rockets extending in front of our army, was repeatedly difcharged with great effect.   The fun, obfcured by duft and fmoke, was in the meridian, and the heat exceffive.   At length our troops, grown impatient from the galling of the enemy's cannon, prepared to charge.   This being told me by my brother, who fupported me on the elephant, I raifed myfelf as much as I could, adjufted my armour, and obferved the motions.   I faw Khan Aulum move towards the enemy with great rapidity, upon which I waved my handkerchief as a fignal for the prince Bedar Bukht to follow, which he did, fo that I fhortly could fee only the top of his ⁴ amaury.   As to myfelf, I could not move, being wedged in by the crowd of elephants around me.

---

[1] The rocket in India is ufed in war, and the chamber being made of iron, does execution wherever it ftrikes, but cannot be fent in true direction.   It will reach from three to four hundred yards.

[2] Anglicè, Refpecter of the faith, king poffeffing the world; eldeft fon of Shaw Aulum.

[3] King of the world; youngeft fon of Shaw Aulum.

[4] A canopied feat for an elephant.   An open one is called howzah, or howdah.

5   As

As Khan Aulum advanced nearer the enemy, his followers diminished, gradually lagging behind, and not above three hundred stuck by him to the charge. When I saw this, I well knew that all was loft. The brave chief, however, penetrated to the elephant of Azeem Oofhaun, and hurled his spear at the prince, but it miffed him, and struck the thigh of an attendant; when the prince drew an arrow, which pierced the heart of Khan Aulum, and he died on the inftant. His brother, Munnower Khan, was also wounded. Their followers fell back in the utmoft confufion, and fled, as did the greateft part of our right wing, leaving the prince Wallajah in a manner alone; but, notwithftanding this defertion, he heroically kept his poft. Amaun Oollah Khan, feeing his danger, haftened to fupport him, when unluckily a rocket lighting in the pad fupporting his feat on the elephant, it took fire, and burnt fo furioufly as to pain the animal, who turned back. The khan, half burnt, fell to the ground; and his troops, thinking he was killed, fled in diforder. The prince Wallajah, upon this, retreated for fhelter towards Bedar Bukht.

A body of the enemy, under Bauz Khan Afghan, now attacked Zoolfeccar Khan, but was repulfed with great lofs, and the chief badly wounded; but, by the decrees of Providence, Ram Sing Harra, and Dulput Raow Boñedelah, on whofe valour and conduct Zoolfeccar Khan moft depended, were both killed at the fame inftant by a cannon fhot; upon which their raujepoots loft all confidence, and fled with the dead bodies of their chiefs. Zoolfeccar Khan, however, yet remained firm with his own followers; but, upon being charged by the whole of Azeem Oofhaun's divifion, he left the conduct of the battle to Syed 'Muzuffir, and retired to the rear of Azim Shaw's poft with Hummeed ad Dien Khan, and, having difmounted from his elephant, fled on horfe-

¹ Victorious,

back

back to Gualiar, where he was received by his father, ' Aſſud Khan.
His flight determined the rout of our army.

The principal followers and perſonal attendants of Azim Shaw
now diſmounted, and laying their quivers on the ground, ſat down
to wait the charge of the enemy, and ſell their lives in defence of
their patron.   Syed Abdoolla, and his brother Houſſein Ali Khan,
of the illuſtrious houſe of Barreh, ever celebrated for valour, whoſe
anceſtors had in every reign performed the moſt gallant actions, if
poſſible ſuperior to their ſires, deſcended from their elephants, and
prepared to engage on foot.   The battle now raged hand to hand
with ſabres, and great ſlaughter on both ſides.   Houſſein Ali Khan
received ſeveral wounds, and fell down faint with the loſs of blood.
Amaun Oolla Khan was killed.   Terbeut Khan, Muttullub Khan,
and Khoodabundeh Khan, having expended all their arrows, uſed
their ſabres; but the former was ſoon killed by a muſquet ball, and the
two latter fell down faint with many wounds.   Suffawee Khan, of
the royal houſe of Perſia, Meerza Abdoolla, and a numerous band
of great officers of Azim Shaw, were ſlain, after each had ſhewn the
valour of Rooſtum in his defence.   At laſt a muſquet ball, and
ſeveral arrows, ſtruck the prince Bedar Bukht, and he ſunk down
dead upon his elephant.   I ſaw him fall, and in the agony of grief
exclaimed, " Hadſt thou not, O God, created ambition of crowns
" and thrones, the head of my prince had not been thus humbled
" in duſt and blood !"

Azim Shaw, though much wounded, was ſtill alive, when a
whirl of duſt winded towards him from the army of Shaw Aulum.
From this now iſſued Monauim Khan with a ſelect band, the
princes Azeem Ooſhaun, Moiz ad dien Jehaundar Shaw, and
Jehaun Shaw.   Azim Shaw ſoon received a mortal wound from a

* Anglicè, Lion ; ſignifying like one in valour.

muſquet

mufquet ball, and refigned his foul to the Creator of life. The prince Wallajah alfo funk down in the fleep of death. I now made my efcape towards Agra, not chufing to go to the enemy's camp, though I had many friends, who would have given me protection.

Rooftum dil Khan, who, as already mentioned, commanded the efcort of Shaw Aulum's advanced tents, when attacked in the morning by our troops, finding his efcape cut off, paid his refpects to Azim Shaw, and had continued near his elephant during the battle, till his death, with great firmnefs. Seeing him dead, he afcended the elephant, and cutting off the head of the corpfe, remounted his horfe, and haftened to the camp of Shaw Aulum. With exulting hope of great reward, he laid his prize at the prince's feet; but the compaffionate Shaw Aulum, feeing the head of his flaughtered brother in fuch difgrace, fhed tears of affection, and gave him nothing but reproaches. He ordered the head to be buried with proper refpect, and forbad the march of victory to be beaten.

Monauim Khan took charge of the bodies of the unfortunate princes, and treated the ladies of their harams with the utmoft refpect and tendernefs. Though he had received a dangerous wound, and fuffered extreme pain, he concealed his fituation, and continued on the field till late at night, to reftore order and prevent plunder. He could not difmount from his elephant without help and was obliged, no pallekee being at hand, to be carried in a cloth to the prefence of Shaw Aulum. His eldeft fon, Nyeem Khan, alfo was dangeroufly wounded by a ball in the neck, and was recovered with difficulty. Shaw Aulum paffed the night under a fhaumianeh on the field of battle, and the next day, having attained the important object of empire, with his mind freed from the

8   dread

dread of a rival, moved in triumph to the gardens of [1] Dhera, round which his army encamped.

I shall now relate some particulars necessary to be known concerning Shaw Aulum; his march from Cabul, and other proceedings, to the day of engagement with his unfortunate brother Azim Shaw.

Some time before his death, Aulumgeer had appointed Monauim Khan to be [2] dewan to Shaw Aulum, who then held the government of Cabul. This nobleman was of great abilities, active in the cabinet, resolute in execution, and of unbending integrity of mind. He soon arranged the prince's affairs, which, before his coming into office, were always in confusion, owing to the ascendancy of unworthy favourites. Dissolute and oppressive, they, from self-interested motives, interfered with the duties of a dewan, and prevented him from doing justice. A superfluous soldiery was kept up, exceeding the ability of the revenue, and, being consequently ill paid, was ever mutinous and discontented. At the same time the houshold of the prince was distressed. Monauim Khan, respected from the esteem in which he was held by the emperor, and his already established character of great ability, soon gained the perfect confidence of Shaw Aulum. He diminished the prince's army, but took care to pay that on foot regularly, so as to leave no room for discontent, or excuse for licentiousness. When he had thus reformed affairs at Cabul, he left his son as his deputy there, and removed to Lahore, the collections of which province were full of abuses. He had resolved to amend them, and succeeded, so as to render the majority of all ranks pleased with his administration. When he heard of Aulumgeer's illness, in order

---

[1] About three cofs, or six miles, from Agra.   [2] Manager of the revenues.

to prevent cabals in favour of Azim Shaw, he circulated a report that Shaw Aulum would not contend for empire, but feek protection from his brother by a flight to Perfia. Shaw Aulum had himself, indeed, made this declaration long before; and with fuch apparent refolution, that it was believed, and dreaded even by his fons, who refided with him. Monauim Khan related to me afterwards the following anecdote, in thefe words:

" When I perceived that my attachment, fincerity, and abilities,
" had properly impreffed Shaw Aulum's mind, and that he was
" convinced I was a prudent, faithful and fecret fervant, being
" alone one day with him, converfing on the affairs of the empire,
" I took the liberty of thus addreffing him: *It is reported that your*
" *highnefs intends flying to Perfia, with fo much confidence, that even*
" *the princes, your fons, affure me by facred oaths of its truth.* He
" replied, *In this rumour there lies concealed a great defign, to for-*
" *ward which, I have fpread it abroad, and taken pains to make it*
" *believed. Firft, becaufe my father, on a mere fufpicion of difloyalty,*
" *kept me nine years in clofe confinement; and, fhould he even now*
" *think I cherifhed the fmalleft ambition, he would immediately ftrive*
" *to accomplifh my ruin. Secondly, my brother, Mahummud Azim*
" *Shaw, who is my powerful enemy, and valiant even to the extreme*
" *of rafhnefs, would exert all his force againft me. From this report,*
" *my father is eafy, and my brother lulled into felf-fecurity; but, by*
" *the Almighty God who gave me life,* laying his hand on the Koraun
" by him, *and on this holy book, I fwear, though not one friend fhould*
" *join me, I will meet Azim Shaw in fingle combat, wherever he may*
" *be. This fecret, which I have fo long maintained, and even kept*
" *from my own children, is now entrufted to your care. Be cautious*
" *that no inftance of your conduct may betray it!* "

To proceed. When the news of Aulumgeer's death reached Monauim Khan at Lahore, he wrote immediately by exprefs to Shaw Aulum, conjuring him to march with the utmoft expedition towards the capital, without anxiety or preparation, as he fhould find artillery and all fupplies ready at Lahore. This wife minifter then prepared bridges over the various rivers, fo that not a day's delay was occafioned in croffing to the prince's army, which at Lahore was joined by a powerful train of artillery, with fufficient draft. He alfo paid up all the troops, and advanced large fums to new levies. Shaw Aulum, by long marches of ten and twelve cofs each day, foon arrived in the neighbourhood of Dhely, and Monauim Khan entered that city with a felect party. The officers of Azim Shaw were alarmed, and either fled, or concealed themfelves in difguifes. [1]Mahummud Ear Khan, the kelladar of the palace, a cautious perfon, and ever looking into futurity, though he knew moft of the great ameers had embraced the caufe of Azim Shaw, yet was fo awed with the vizier's gallantry, and the arrival of Shaw Aulum, that he faw no fecurity for himfelf but in refigning his charge. He accordingly gave up the palace, in which were the treafures of Hindoftan, collected from the reign of Akber to the prefent times. Thus was Shaw Aulum, by the activity and refolution of his fervant, made mafter of funds to fupport (if he chofe) all the troops to be levied in the empire. The army was now increafed to one hundred thoufand horfe, and foldiers of every caft and fect flocked in crowds to the imperial ftandard, where they were received with proper encouragement and amply paid. Monauim Khan advanced with fome chofen troops before the prince to Agra, and though Bedar Bukht was at the Chumbul, and Azim Shaw arrived at Gualiar, he was not alarmed, but encamped immediately before the citadel. [2]Baukee Khan, an old imperial fer-

---

[1] Anglicè, Friend of Mahummud.   [2] Anglicè, Conftant.

vant,

vant, and governor of the fortrefs, which he had refufed to refign to Azeem Oofhawn, being certified that Shaw Aulum was approaching, did not chufe to refift longer, but fent offers, that if Monauim Khan would come firft alone into the citadel, he would refign the command. He accordingly, without the leaft diftruft, entered over a narrow plank, only paffable for a fingle perfon, which was placed over a deep ditch from a fmall wicket to admit him. As he had made a forced march from Muttra, of twenty cofs, he now lay down to take a few hours reft, till all his followers arrived. After this refrefhment, he fealed up the treafury, pofted his people at the different gates, and about midnight went to vifit Azeem Oofhawn, who was encamped at the diftance of fix cofs, to whom he offered much friendly advice for his conduct to his father, who was jealous of his loyalty. When the news of the furrender of the citadel of Agra reached Bedar Bukht at ' Dholepore, his fpirit was broken, and the crimfon of his hopes faded into pale defpair. I was with him at the time, and perceived that he regarded every thing as loft. He immediately fent an account of the event to his father, who had not yet heard of Shaw Aulum's arrival at Muttra, as his weak fervants, fearful of his difpleafure, and the ufual grofs abufe, dared not to inform him. At length Shaw Aulum made the propofal of a divifion of the empire, which was refufed, and two days afterwards the conflict enfued, as above-mentioned.

Without doubt, Shaw Aulum's fucceffes, and his attainment of the empire, were owing to the conduct and valour of this great minifter; yet he never fet forth himfelf as having done any extra-ordinary fervice, but would often fay to his majefty, that empire was the particular gift of God, and that no obligation could be

' A town on the bank of the Chumbul, in the province of Agra.

laid

laid on fovereigns; fo that, if any one thought himfelf conducive
to their fuccefs, it was, in them, vanity and folly. To me, from
whom he kept not his inmoft thoughts, he would fay, " Kings,
" through the blaze of fplendor, cannot fee impartially; therefore,
" if any perfon prefumes upon fervices, and would fhew that he
" thinks them an obligation on his mafter, the jealous difpofition
" of royalty cannot bear it, and rejects the claim, as was clearly
" proved in the proceedings of the emperor Mahummud Akber,
" and ¹ Beyram Khan, his affuming minifter."

It is now neceffary to fay fomething of the four fons of Shaw
Aulum, their difpofitions and behaviour, both in public and private.

² Moiz ad Dien Jehaundaur Shaw, the eldeft, was a weak man,
devoted to pleafure, who gave himfelf no trouble about ftate affairs,
or to gain the attachment of any of the nobility, as will be feen
when I come to relate his reign.

Azeem Oofhawn, the fecond fon, was a ftatefman of winning
manners. Aulumgeer had always purfued the policy of encou-
raging his grandfons, and employing them in public affairs; for,
as his fons were ambitious, of great power, and at the head of
armies, he thus prudently controuled them, by oppofing to them
enemies in their own families, as Bedar Bukht to Azim Shaw, and
Azeem Oofhawn to Shaw Aulum. To the latter he had given the
advantageous government of the three provinces of Bengal, Bahar,
and Oriffa, from whence he had now come with a rich treafure,

---

¹ Eeyram Khan, on the death of Humaioon, became regent during the minority of
Akber, who, at the age of feventeen, not chufing longer to be governed by a fubject,
difplaced him.
² Anglicè, Refpecter of the faith.

and confiderable army; and though in the late battle he had performed great fervice, yet he was fufpected by his father, and dreaded as a rival: but to relate the caufes would be ufelefs prolixity.

[1] Ruffeh Oofhawn, the private companion and favourite of his father, was a prince of quick parts, a great proficient in religious learning, a fine writer, and of much knowledge in the law, but at the fame time addicted to pleafure, particularly fond of mufic, and the pomp of courtly fhew. He paid no attention to public affairs, or even thofe of his own houfhold.

[2] Khojefteh Akhter Jehaun Shaw had the greateft fhare of all the princes in the management of affairs, before his father's acceffion to the throne; after which, the whole adminiftration of the empire was long influenced by him. He had the clofeft friendfhip and connection with Monauim Khan, who, by his intereft, was appointed vizier.

When Shaw Aulum had repofed from the fatigues of war, he took meafures to reduce Kaum Bukfh, who had affumed the imperial titles in Dekkan. It was not fuppofed that he could make much oppofition, but in the opinions of the wife and underftanding prejudged, that his behaviour would of itfelf ruin him in that country.

Monauim Khan now called together, by attention and confoling behaviour, the unfortunate nobility of Azim Shaw, who had efcaped from the late battle to different places. Zoolfeccar Khan had fled to his father, [3] Affud Khan, who had the charge of Azim

---

[1] Anglicè, Of high rank.
[2] Of happy ftar; king of the world.
[3] Anglicè, Lion.

Shaw's

Shaw's baggage in Gualiar. The vizier had taken pains to convince his mafter, that the ancient nobility were the pillars of the ftate, and that the welfare of the empire depended on their perfons, whofe anceftors had held high offices, and acquired influence and refpect with the people, fo that it was proper and politic to employ them.

As the vizarut had been conferred on Monauim Khan, at his requeft, the moft dignified office of ¹ vakeel muttulluk was entrufted to Affud Khan, and that of ² meer bukfhi to his fon Zoolfeccar Khan, with the title of Ameer al Amra. The fecond bukhfhifhip was conferred on Meerza Shawnowaz Khan Suffawee. Monauim Khan, regardlefs of trifles, fubmitted to fit below Affud Khan in the divans, and to fhew him every refpect as his fuperior in office. The government of all Dekkan was granted to the ameer al amra Zoolfeccar Khan, who performed the duties by his deputy, Daood Khan Punnee, while he in perfon attended the court.

Monauim Khan, fincerely loyal, generous in mind, and full of zeal for the fervice of his mafter, never preferred the gratification of his own paffions to the welfare of the ftate, or honour of the fovereign. He both advifed and acted what was for his glory. For example, moft of the ameers of Aulumgeer had accompanied Azim Shaw, and fought againft Shaw Aulum in the late conteft, confequently were liable in juftice to whatever evils or punifhments he chofe to inflict upon them; but Monauim Khan became their general interceffor, reprefenting to the emperor, that they were

¹ Anglicè, Univerfal agent. This is an office fuperior to that of vizier. It is feldom filled up, but in time of great emergency; but it was lately conferred on the infant Peifhwa, by his prefent majefty of Dhely, though it cannot be confidered now but as an empty honour. It feems to have been no more to Affud Khan.

² Chief paymafter.

³ Anglicè, Favoured by the king.

excufable,

excufable, having only obeyed an heir who fat upon the throne, which, as affairs were circumftanced at that time, they could not avoid; that, after they had become his friends, [1] eaten of his falt, and made new compacts and declarations in addition to their former vows of allegiance, they could not in honour abufe his confidence by treachery or defertion. He obferved, that the empire of Hindoftan was a ftate not to be kept in order by one or two perfons; that, like the magnificent pavilion of [2] Soleymaun, many ftrong pillars and powerful cords were required to fupport it, and keep it on a lafting footing; that the noble families, who from generation to generation had the benefit of experience, a knowledge of the cuftoms of the empire and rules of government, were alone fuited to high employments; that moft of the prefent nobility had alfo held for many years important offices, and acquired wifdom and knowledge. He faid, that, if they were not ftill entrufted with the pofts of greateft confidence, there would not remain a poffibility of fupporting the rules of the empire, or obtaining able ftatefmen or good generals. He advifed his majefty to reward amply thofe perfons who had joined his ftandard from every quarter, and done good fervices, agreeable to their merits; but without exalting them beyond their abilities, obferving that many of them had only been dependants on the princes and nobility, others again only fervants to fojedaurs and governors of towns. Where then could they have acquired judgment in politics and knowledge of government, dignity of manner, or fortitude to fupport the power of command? He obferved, that fuch accomplifhments were inherent to noble birth and liberal education, the natural confequence of fuch advantage. Such was the vizier, of whofe mafter (worthy of him) I now fpeak.

[1] This expreffion implies a very ftrong connection in the original idiom.

[2] According to Mahummedan tradition, Solomon had a very fumptuous pavilion made for him by the Genii.

Shaw

Shaw Aulum was generous and merciful, of a great foul tempered with affability, difcerning of merit. He had feen the ftrict exercife of power during the reigns of his grandfather and father, and been ufed to authority himfelf for the laft fifty years. Time received a new luftre from his acceffion, and all ranks of people obtained favours equal, if not fuperior, to their merits; fo that the public forgot the excellencies and great qualities of Aulumgeer, which became abforbed in the bounties of his fucceffor. Some narrow-hearted perfons, however, out of ingratitude and envy, attributed his general liberality to ill-placed extravagance and pro-fufion; but it is a fact, that the deferving of every profeffion, and worthy of all degrees, whether among the learned or the eloquent, the noble or the ignoble, received an attention from the throne, which the eye of time prior to this had never feen, nor had fuch been heard of before by the ears of fame. His perfonal qualities and perfections, fpeech is unequal to relate. His valour was fuch, that he had refolved on meeting Azim Shaw, whofe bravery was celebrated, in fingle combat. His four fons, poffeffed of great power and confiderable force, he fuffered conftantly to be near his perfon, never giving himfelf a moment's fufpicion regarding them, nor preventing their forming connections with the prime nobility; upon which fubject I, the humbleft of his flaves, once ventured to prefent him a petition of a cautionary nature, thinking it my duty, as I had often done fo to Aulumgeer. To what I reprefented, he wrote a wife and juft reply, which, by God's permiffion, I will one time or other relate. He permitted the fons of thofe princes, who had fallen in battle againft him, to appear at all times com-pletely armed in his prefence. The infant children he let remain unmolefted with their mothers, while thofe arrived at manhood daily accompanied him in the chace, unguarded, and fhared in all his diverfions. His court was magnificent to a degree beyond that of Shaw Jehaun. Seventeen princes, his fons, grandfons, and

nephews,

nephews, fat generally round his throne, in the manner following:
—On his right hand, Jehaundaur Shaw, his eldeft fon, with his
three fons, his third fon Ruffeh Ooſhawn with his three fons, and
Bedar Dil, fon to his nephew Bedar Bukht. On his left, Mahummud Azeem Ooſhawn with his two fons, and Jehaun Shaw with
his fon. ¹Ali Tibbar, the only furviving fon of Azim Shaw, fat
on the right hand of Azeem Ooſhawn, and a little to the right,
fomewhat advanced, the two fons of Mahummud Kaum Bukſh.
Behind the royal princes, on the right, ſtood the fons of conquered
fovereigns, as of Secunder Adil Shaw of Beejapore, and Koottub
Shaw, king of Golconda; alfo a vaft crowd of the nobility, from
the rank of feven to three thoufand, fuch as were allowed to be on
the platform between the filver rails. How can I mention every
particular of the fplendid fcene? On the ²eeds, and other feftivals,
his majefty, with his own hands, gave the betel and perfumes to
all in his prefence, according to their ranks. His gifts of jewels,
dreffes, and other favours, were truly royal. When in private, he
dreffed plain and humbly, like a religious, and daily, without fail,
prayed with many in company. Frequently on holidays and Fri-
days, when travelling, he would read the prayers himfelf, in the

---

¹ Anglicè, Of high defcent.

² The Mahummedans have two grand eeds or holidays, one at the conclufion of
the ramzaun, and the other on the anniverfary of the day on which Abraham confented
to facrifice his fon. On thefe days, tents are pitched about a mile diftant from the
city, to which the emperor goes in great ftate to pray, and on his return receives
prefents from his ameers, on whom he confers honorary dreffes according to rank.
The fame ceremony is obferved in every town, by the governor. At the laft eede,
after prayers, a camel is facrificed, and a fmall part of it dreffed, and eaten on the fpot
by the emperor and his attendants. The cavalcades which I chanced to attend on
each of thefe days, at Lucnow and Banaris, were very brilliant, and ferved to give an
idea of the aftonifhing fplendor which muft have graced thefe in the flourifhing times
of the empire. It is probable Mr. Zoffani may offer the public a view of the proceffion
at Lucnow, on the firft eed in 1784, as he was prefent, and took a fketch of it.

H   grand

grand tent of audience, and repeat portions of the Koraun with a
tone and fweetnefs which captivated the moft eloquent Arabians.
He never miffed the devotions of the latter part of the night, and
frequently employed the whole in prayer.   In the early part of the
evening, he had generally an affembly of the religious, or learned
men.   He himfelf related ¹ traditions, in the number of which he
excelled, as well as in a knowledge of the holy laws.   He had ex-
plored the different opinions of all fects, read the works of all
free-thinkers, and was well acquainted with the hypothefes of each.
On this account, fome over-ftrict devotees accufed him of hetero-
doxy in his religious opinions, through mere envy of his fuperior
abilities.   I heard moft of his tenets, and lamented the infolence
of his vain critics; for it was as clear as the fun, how juft and
orthodox he was in his opinions on religious points.   But how can
I enumerate all his perfections! It would fill volumes to recite but
a fmall part; therefore I fhall defift, and now relate, as briefly as
poffible, the expedition of his majefty to Dekkan, againft the
death-devoted Kaum Bukfh.

It has been already mentioned that the late emperor; a few days
before his death, difpatched Kaum Bukfh to Beejapore.   This
prince was of an excellent memory, learned, and a pleafing writer,
poffeffed of all outward accomplifhments in a high degree; but
there was in his mind a flightinefs that approached near to infanity.
He feldom remained a month in his father's prefence, but, for fome
mifbehaviour, he was reproved, degraded, or confined; and fome
acts were done by him, to mention which would be unworthy of
me.   When he arrived at Beejapore, he immediately proclaimed
himfelf in the ² khootba, and ftruck coins in his own name.   What
follies

¹ Anecdotes and maxims of the prophet.

² The khootba is a form of prayer, in which the fouls of all departed patriarchs and
prophets are firft prayed for, beginning with Adam, and ending with Mahummud.
The fouls of the reigning family's anceftors are then recommended to mercy, and the

follies was he not guilty of, from the madnefs of his mind, and the confidence he put in lying vifionaries! Thefe wretches had hailed each of the princes with a prophecy of fucceffion to the throne, fwearing they had converfations in their reveries with God, his prophet, and the pious faints, who had promifed their affift- ance, fo that human force was unneceffary. They affured Kaum Bukfh, that he need not levy any troops for his fupport; for, though an enemy fhould march againft him with all the myriads of ' Toor and Sullum, they would not dare to face his fight, much lefs engage in battle. Flattered by this, and impelled by madnefs, the weak youth regarded himfelf as emperor, and invincible in his fingle perfon; to prove which, he would often relate, in a raving manner, ftrange prognoftics and divine greetings fhewn to himfelf. His prophets having told him, that his eldeft fon would alfo one time become emperor, he became jealous of the innocent child, and frequently meditated to put him to death, but was withheld from that crime by the dread he had of Aulumgeer: however, he kept him conftantly in confinement, miferably clothed, and worfe fed than the fon of a wretched beggar, which was worfe than death. From the fame caufe, on ill-placed fufpicions, he inflicted tortures and uncommon punifhments on the ladies of his haram, putting many of them privately to death. To his fervants, companions, and confidants, he often behaved with outrageous cruelty, doing fuch acts to them as before eye never faw, nor ear had heard.

Notwithftanding thefe blots in his character, as he was a fon of Aulumgeer, and that part of the empire had been given to him, at firft moft of the chiefs of Dekkan, whether Muffulmauns or Hin-

---

whole concludes with a prayer for the profperity of the monarch on the throne, and the welfare of his fubjects. It is read every Friday in the mizid jamée, or grand mofque of all towns, and on the eeds or grand feftivals.

' Two great hofts, mentioned in the Koraun.

doos,

doos, crowded to his ftandard, and the Imperial officers, as Syef Khan, Rooftum Dil Khan, and others of all ranks, joined in acknowledging him emperor. Leaving his fofter-brother, Meer Mullung, a debauched youth of neither birth or merit, at Beejapore as governor, he marched himfelf to Hyderabad, then commanded by Rooftum Dil Khan, who had fucceeded his father, [1] Jan-fippar Khan, by Aulumgeer's orders, in that government. In this province he reduced fome powerful zemindars to his obedience, and difplaced others.

[2] Ghazee ad Dien Khan Bahadar Firofe Jung, who had acquired a moft powerful influence in Dekkan, was chief of the Tooranee moguls, and kept on foot a great army, had withdrawn himfelf from Azim Shaw. He was alfo much in dread of Shaw Aulum's refentment, he having advifed that prince's being confined, when Aulumgeer was before Golconda. The late emperor had ftrenuoufly endeavoured to attach the Tooranees to Kaum Bukfh, and for this purpofe had appointed for that prince's preceptor, Syed Oughlan Seyadut Khan, the agent at court, and bofom confidant of Ghazee ad Dien Khan, venerated alfo by all the Toranees of every rank. He had alfo charged them with the protection of his perfon; but fuch was the temper of the unhappy prince, that at a time like this, when he claimed the throne, and, favourably for his caufe, Ghazee ad Dien Khan dreaded Shaw Aulum, he could not make him his friend: on the contrary, he did many acts to difpleafe him, and excite his alarms. This chief was an able ftatefman of long experience, who, though blind of fight, could clearly perceive the mind of man; therefore, whatever wifhes he might have to enjoy the honour of making an emperor, yet he foon faw the follies of Kaum Bukfh, and declined his caufe, as ruinous and

[1] Anglicè, Life-refigning.
[2] Anglicè, Champion of the faith; valiant and fortunate in war.

8

loft.

loft. In a fhort time too, the chief zemindars of Dekkan, who had in general joined his ftandard, difpleafed at his conduct and heedlefs fhedding of human blood, his inconftancy of mind and breach of treaties, left him, and retired to their own countries, where they took care to fecure themfelves, till the difputes for the throne fhould be decided.

Thus, though the pretenfions of Kaum Bukfh were of no great importance, yet he was a fon of Aulumgeer, and claimed a right to the empire. The behaviour of Ghazee ad Dien Khan alfo demanded confideration. 'Ajeet Sing, hereditary zemindar of Jodepore, and Jey Sing, of Ambeer, did not fhew that obedience and refpect to the throne which had been obferved by their anceftors, and meditated rebellion. All thefe circumftances made his majefty refolve on marching to Dekkan. The 'khan khanan opened a correfpondence with Ghazee ad Dien Khan, to whom he gave much confolation, affurances of favour, and friendly advice. That experienced ftatefman, opening his eyes on the viciffitudes of life, faw it was his intereft, if his majefty would forget the paft, and not moleft him in his fortune, to bend his head in fubmiffion, and retire from bufinefs to a life of devotion. His only fon, 'Cheen Koolich Khan, had long difagreed with him, and his brother, 'Hamid Khan, whom he had appointed his deputy in command of the troops, had feparated from him, and gone over to the prefence. The Tooran chiefs of his houfhold alfo, when they faw his fortunes on the decline, had left his fervice. All thefe events

' Son of the celebrated Jeffwunt Sing, who acted fo capital a part in the competitions of Aulumgeer and his brothers.
' Lord of Lords. Monauim Khan is meant by this title, which he received from Shaw Aulum.
' Anglicè, Sword-drawing lord. He was afterwards famous as Nizam al Mulluck.
' Anglicè, Affifting.

made

made him glad to embrace the promifes of the minifter, and thankfully accept the foubadacy of Ahmedabad Guzarat. He accordingly croffed the Nerbudda, and left Dekkan without trouble, but his fears prevented his coming to the court. He had not been in that of Aulumgeer fince his lofs of fight, which that generous and forgiving prince, out of regard to his former fervices, and from motives of policy, had excufed.

Shaw Aulum began his march to Dekkan with an army fuperior to that of any of the former emperors, and a fplendor till now unfeen, having in his train all the princes, and a great concourfe of nobility of every rank. The prudent and able Monauim Khan took fuch meafures for the fupplies of this mighty force, exceeding Aulumgeer's by an hundred thoufand men, that the emperor had no trouble or difficulty, though only in the beginning of his reign, when the revenues of the provinces had not yet been received, nor refpect for the throne been properly impreffed in different quarters. When his majefty had arrived at Aurungabad, before he would advance towards Hyderabad, where the frantic Kaum Bukfh then was, he wrote him feveral kind letters and friendly admonitions, to this effect :—" Our ever-honoured father refigned to you only " Beejapore ; but we give you, in addition, Hyderabad. Thefe " two extenfive countries, long famous for their great kings, pro- " ducing a revenue more than half of Hindoftan, we leave to you, " without interference or reluctance, and fhall efteem you dearer " than our own children. Think not then of contention, nor " confent to fhed the blood of the faithful, nor difturb the repofe " of our government. If you give the ear of acceptance to this " advice, we will farther confer upon you the nizamut of Dekkan, " if agreeable to you ; and, after vifiting the facred tomb of our " father, we will return to Hindoftan."

There

There was no treachery or deceit in this generous offer, for Shaw Aulum always fhewed tendernefs, liberality and affection, in his conduct to his brothers. Kaum Bukfh, weak and felf-conceited as a child, bent on error, paid not the fmalleft attention to his brother, and continued to add frefh affronts to his authority. Rooftum Dil Khan, Syef Khan of the Imperial fervants, and others of no family or note, on whom he had beftowed titles of nobility, with about twenty thoufand horfe and foot, were now with him, but, difgufted at his behaviour, meditated opportunities to quit him. Monauim Khan, with his ufual prudence, had fent them letters, affuring them of the emperor's forgivenefs and favour; fo that all, even to Meer Mullung, Kaum Bukfh's fofter-brother, had refolved to come over, and embrace his protection; but the prince, fufpecting their intentions, put to death Rooftum Dil Khan, Syef Khan, and Meer Mullung, and plundered their families of all they poffeffed, on the fame day, and in the fame place. He had after this no officer of confequence with him, and his treafure being expended, all his troops deferted, except about ten thoufand of the worft Dekkan horfe, and his fmall artillery; yet he ftill refolved to hazard a battle. When Shaw Aulum arrived within twelve cofs of Hyderabad, the unfortunate Kaum Bukfh loft daily his followers in crowds, and moft of the zemindars of Dekkan retired to their homes; while the remainder mutinied for arrears, and hourly threatened to plunder his effects. Will it be believed, that he yet determined to refift, and expected victory? He even quitted the afylum of the city walls, and encamped upon a plain about the diftance of three cofs, with his fmall force, within fight of the emperor's army; fo great was his enthufiaftic belief in the prophecies of his deceiving, and perhaps felf-deceived, devotees.

Shaw Aulum, from compaffion to his brother, and the hope of yet reducing him by gentle means, would not permit his troops to attack;

attack; but Kaum Bukſh interpreted the inactivity of the Imperial army into fear, from his belief that the prophecies in his favour were now on the point of accompliſhment; for he had been aſſured by viſionaries, that, though alone, mighty hoſts would never prevail againſt him. Accordingly, though deſerted by almoſt all his followers, he yet obſtinately refuſed to pay allegiance to his brother. At length the ameer al amra Zoolfeccar Khan, who had a keen enmity againſt the miſguided prince, and wiſhed to ſhew his zeal

A.H. 1120.
A.C. 1708.

for his new patron, reſolved to ſeize him. He accordingly obtained leave to march, under the pretence of reconnoitring the enemy, and moved towards him with his own followers, a diviſion from the troops of Monauim Khan, and a body of Mharattas under the chief Neema Sindia. The unfortunate prince prepared to withſtand ſuch ſuperior force; but, being charged at once on all ſides, was inſtantly deſerted by all his followers, except a few perſonal attendants. Notwithſtanding this, he continued, as long as he had ſtrength, to uſe his bow and arrows from his elephant, till at length he ſunk down on his ſeat, through loſs of blood from ſeveral wounds. He was then taken priſoner by Daood Khan, and carried to the prince Jehaun Shaw, who, with his brothers, had ſtood at ſome diſtance during this extraordinary ſkirmiſh.

The captive prince was conveyed immediately to the Imperial tents, and being laid upon a bed in the ¹ tuſhbeh khaneh, near the private apartments, was viſited by his brother, the emperor, who endeavoured to comfort him by every expreſſion of affectionate concern. The phyſicians and ſurgeons alſo attended, but he would not allow his wounds to be dreſſed, though earneſtly entreated by his majeſty and his ſons. He ſpoke but little; but when the prince Ruffeh Ooſhawn tenderly aſked, why he had refuſed offers of

_____
¹ An oratory, where prayers are ſaid.

favour,

favour, he replied, " His majefty was very gracious; but how " could I fubmit to meet him in any other way than this?" Upon Jehaun Shaw's repeating the queftion, he exclaimed, " I have " done wrong; do not you follow my example !" One of the princes afking him if he had more than a thoufand followers when taken, he angrily anfwered, " No ; but had there been lefs than " five hundred, I could with equal eafe have brought myfelf here." He then turned to the emperor, and faid, " There are, in a cafket " upon my elephant, fome jewels of our father and my own, of " which I beg your majefty's acceptance." After this he grew faint, and languifhed in filence, without uttering a fingle groan, till nine at night, when he refigned his foul to the Creator of life. We are from God, and to God we muft return.

When Shaw Aulum had thus fuccefsfully concluded the war with his brother, he did not chufe to remain longer in Dekkan, though the affairs of that country required much arrangement, to infure its future dependance on the empire. Perhaps he dreaded the fate of his father, who, after the reduction of Beejapore, Hyderabad, and the taking of Sambah, remained to finifh fome objects which then appeared eafily attainable, but afterwards extended in fuch a chain, that he could not quit Dekkan for the remainder of his life. He had often lamented this neceffity, and the relaxation which his abfence occafioned in the government of Hindoftan; and would frequently fay to his confidants in private, " My difloyal " fubjects have impofed upon me this play-thing, that they may " enjoy commands and honours." But I am wandering from my fubject. Shaw Aulum, in the height of the rains, began his march from Hyderabad, leaving as deputy-governor of Dekkan, Daood Khan Punnee, a native of the country, and a nobleman of great military fame. When he recroffed the Nerbudda, it was intended to employ all the powers of government to fettle, in a proper

I

manner,

manner, the Rajapoote countries, which had been difaffected ever
fince the acceffion of Aulumgeer; who, though offended at the
behaviour of the rajas Ajeet Sing and Jey Sing, over whofe terri-
tories he had appointed Imperial governors, yet was not able, from
the wars in Dekkan, to punifh them effectually. They had indeed
vifited Shaw Aulum, but had left his camp without permiffion, and
now openly fhewed their defigns to ftruggle for independence, in
clofe alliance with each other; to bind which, Jey Sing had efpoufed
the daughter of Ajeet Sing.   At this crifis, intelligence arrived that
the [1] Siks had rifen in rebellion.   This fect of infidels, known alfo
by the names of Nannukkea and Gooroh, had long been eftablifhed
in the foubah of Lahore, by a teacher ftyled Nannuk.   Of his defcendants was the prefent chief, to whom had flocked great crowds
of all ranks, refigning to his difpofal, with blind fidelity, their lives
and properties.   Thus fupported, he excited fedition, and took
arms to extend his errors, and overturn the bafis of the true faith.
He engaged Vizier Khan, the fojedaur of [2] Sirhind, who was killed
in the action, with numbers of his followers; after which the
gooroh poffeffed himfelf of the town of Sirhind, and many diftricts
of Doaub, as far as [3] Boreah, Saarunpore, and Shawdourah, on
both banks of the river Jumnah, where he committed unlimited
exceffes, razing all public edifices, as mofques, colleges, maufoleums, and palaces, killing or taking prifoners the faithful of every
age and fex, and plundering with the moft cruel feverity.   The
oppreffions of thefe wretches were every day increafing, and there
was no nobleman daring enough to march from Dhely againft them.
Afoph ad Dowlah Affud Khan, who governed that capital, fhewing

[1] They now poffefs the provinces of Lahore, Multan, and part of Dhely, plundering as far fouth annually as Rohilcund.

[2] A confiderable town, about fifty cofs N. of Dhely.

[3] Thefe diftricts are now held by Zabtah Khan, a Rohilla chief, who however pays
a tribute to the Siks, and it is faid has entered into their fect.

I   great

great figns of fear, the inhabitants were alarmed, and began to fly, with their families and effects, towards the eaftern provinces, for fhelter from the impending ftorm. All this being reprefented to the emperor, in the higheft colours, his majefty thought it beft to march in perfon againft the infurgents : for this reafon, he refolved for the prefent to lay afide the defign of totally expelling the raja-pootes, and to confirm their allegiance, by winking at their of-fences, till a more convenient opportunity of punifhment. Thefe zemindars had, for generations, been ufed to obey, and had not, in fact, either fortitude or ability to oppofe openly the emperor of Hindoftan, whofe appearance againft them in arms would have been fufficient to curb their infolence ; but the khankhanan, alarmed at the infurrection of the Siks, did not properly reflect on that circumftance, and defcended to fhew the rajapootes fuch favours as were inconfiftent with good policy, as well as the dignity of the fovereign : but he was not alone to blame, as there were other agents in this bufinefs. The four princes were conftantly intriguing againft each other, to obtain influence in the management of public affairs, which occafioned much delay and confufion in bufinefs, fo that the khankhanan thought it happy to fteer his veffel fafe through four fuch 'great feas ; and could not act fo independently for the public good as he wifhed, being obliged to attend to the capricious interefts of others, among which he found it difficult to preferve his own. Among the remarkable occurrences of the expedition into Dekkan, was the decline of Jehaun Shaw's influence with his father, and the rife of that of Azeem Oofhawn, of whom till now the emperor had ever been fufpicious. The prince Jehaun Shaw was of haughty and independent fpirit, ready to take fire on the fmalleft neglect. This, with the behaviour of his fervants, alarmed and difpleafed the khankhanan, who, for his own fafety, watched

---

' Meaning the power and influence of the four princes.

an

an opportunity to deftroy his influence in public affairs: a talk of no great difficulty, to one well acquainted with the difpofition of Shaw Aulum, almoft equally warm with his fon, who had more than once difpleafed him by his behaviour, fo that he had expreffed to him his diffatisfaction. The prince, upon this, thought to prove his difintereftednefs and independence, by neglecting to frequent the durbar, and engage in bufinefs as ufual. Azeem Oofhawn, who had reaped experience in office, and was well verfed in the intrigues of a court, perceiving coolnefs taking place between Jehaun Shaw and the khankhanan, paid fo much flattering attention to the latter, that by degrees he gained his confidence. This gave ftill more offence to Jehaun Shaw, who had too much pride to expoftulate, but neglected the minifter in return. He foon after fell fick, and his indifpofition continuing a long time, gave Azeem Oofhawn ample opportunity of acquiring influence over Shaw Aulum, and the favourites whom his majefty trufted with the fulleft confidence; while he continued to be pleafed with them, but, on the fmalleft difguft, or in their fhorteft abfence, he forgot them altogether.

Azeem Oofhawn having thus gained the credit he aimed at with his father and the minifter, employed it in foftening the rigour of government againft thofe who laboured under its difpleafure; thinking that, thus obliged by his mediation, they would readily return his favours, by embracing his caufe, whenever the death of his father fhould give him a claim to the empire. It was from this hope, that he advifed indulgence to the refractory rajas, and condefcended to repair to their camp, and conduct them from thence to his father, permitting them to be accompanied by all their troops armed. Such unufual indulgence was far from anfwering the end expected by the prince, who fhould have feen, that it could only tend to difplay publickly the fears of government, and confequently

muft

muft reflect difhonour on its advifer, and render him weak in the eyes even of thofe to whom fuch uncommon honours were allowed. In fhort, the two rajas, attended by all their followers, paid their refpects to his majefty on the line of march, were gratified with his affent to whatever their infolence demanded, and difmiffed to their homes with rich prefents and affurances of favour.

When this affair was finifhed, the emperor marched without delay towards Lahore, not even ftopping to make an entrance either at Agra or Dhely. In a fhort time he arrived at Sirhind, which the rebels deferted on his approach, and retired to [1] Daber, the original refidence of their goorroh or chief, where they fortified themfelves as ftrongly as poffible. Though this infurrection was not of fuch importance as to difturb the general repofe of the empire, yet his majefty, defender of the faith, hearing that the malice of the rebels was directed at religion, thought it his duty to go againft them in perfon; in this, copying the example of Aulumgeer, who, in the latter part of his reign, appeared at the fiege of every fort belonging to unbelievers; otherwife, what ability had a wretched and infatuated rabble to dare the prefence of fuch a glorious monarch? The exertions of one of the principal ameers, or, at all events, of the princes, would have been equal to the extinction of the rebellion, and explofion of the fchifm.

The imperial army foon arrived within fight of the goorroh's camp, which lay round the walls of Daber on different heights, commanding the paffes to that fortrefs, fituated on a fummit, fur-rounded by hollows, craggy rocks, and deep paths. Shaw Aulum had refolved to lie inactive before the enemy for fome time, in hopes by this to render them confident, and tempt them to an

[1] At the entrance of the Sewalic mountains, which connect Hindoftan with Thibet.

engagement;

engagement; on which account he iffued pofitive orders to the princes and all the ameers, not to advance nearer the goorroh's lines on any pretence, however favourable. Some days paffed in inactivity, when at length the khankhanan entreated permiffion of his majefty to advance, with his own followers, to reconnoitre the enemy's pofition: which was granted, on condition that he fhould not commence an attack without further orders from the prefence. However, when he had arrived within fhot of their lines, the enemy began a warm cannonade from their works, while bodies of their infantry on the heights galled him with rockets, mufquetry, and arrows. His foldiers, enraged, were not now to be reftrained; and the khankhanan, more jealous of his military fame than fearful of the emperor's difpleafure, ventured for once to difobey, by giving directions to attack. He difmounted from his horfe, and led his brave troops on foot up the moft difficult heights, driving the rebels from them with the greateft rapidity and fuccefs. This fcene paffing within fight of the royal camp, the chiefs and foldiers, emulous of glory, waited not for orders, but haftened to join the attack in great numbers; while the emperor and the four princes viewed the fight from the fquares of their encampments, with a mixture of anger and fatisfaction. At laft the enemy were driven from all their works, to the narrow fummit round the fort of Daber, where they continued to defend themfelves in a defperate manner, but without even the hope of efcape from general flaughter; when night coming on, rendered friends and foes undif-tinguifhable to each other. The khankhanan, fure of having the goorroh in his power, gave orders for his troops to ceafe the attack, and lie upon their arms in their prefent pofition, till the morning fhould enable him to finifh it with fuccefs. He had, however, unluckily neglected to block up a narrow path leading from the fort to the hills, either becaufe he had not perceived it, or was fatisfied that it could not lead but to where the Imperial troops were pofted.

posted. The goorroh, a man of great art, generally appeared in the dress and splendor of a prince, when he wished to be public; but, if occasion required privacy, he disguised himself in the habit of [1] a jogie or synassee, in such a manner, that few, even among his own people, could know him. During the night, he, without acquainting his followers of his intentions, changed his habit, and left the fort undiscovered. The khankhanan, about dawn, renewed the attack, and gained the place, after a short struggle, sword in hand, exulting in the certainty of carrying the goorroh dead or alive to the emperor, whose displeasure at his disobedience of orders, would by this service be changed to approbation : but who can relate his weight of grief and disappointment, at finding that his promised prize had escaped, without leaving a trace behind him ? The goorroh's speed of foot was uncommon, and he only acquainted with the paths and mazes through the hills that led to the snowy mountains, which he had marked for shelter. The khankhanan lost for an instant almost the use of his faculties, which were absorbed in dread of the emperor's anger, not without reason. As he was, agreeable to custom after an important victory, beating the march of triumph in his way to the royal tents, orders arrived, commanding him to stop the drums, and not dare to enter the presence. He retired, drowned in despair, to his own tents; where he had the cruel mortification of learning every instant, from messengers, that his enemies exulted in his fall from favour, and openly condemned his conduct with malicious zeal in the presence of his majesty, who was highly enraged against him. But though this did not continue long, and Shaw Aulum, regarding his former services, received him again into favour, after a few days, yet this noble and faithful minister never recovered from the effects of the royal ingratitude. This grief, added to the pain he

---

[1] Sects of fakeers, or religious mendicants.

felt

felt at feeing three of the princes and the ameer al amra ufing all
arts to complete his ruin, ftuck like a poifoned arrow in his breaft.
He loft all fatisfaction from worldly enjoyments, the emptinefs of
which he now fo fully experienced, and from the day of his difgrace
declined in his health; fo that not long after he was reduced to
keep his bed, where he lingered a few days, and then refigned his
foul to the angel of death; who never, in the uncounted ages of
his office, feized on a foul more pure, or lefs defiled with the frail-
ties of human nature.

A.H. 1124.
A.C. 1712.

While Shaw Aulum, juft as a fovereign, and liberal as a man,
reigned over the empire with a gentle hand, in perfect repofe, Providence was preparing new revolutions, and Time haftening to
difclofe events of dreadful importance. The bloffoms numeroufly
fhooting under the influence of the Imperial fpring, were deftined
to be blafted by the ftorms of autumn, and only one unkindly fruit
to remain on the royal tree. A deadly vapour, poifonous as the
piercing venom of the fnake, all at once infected the head and heart
of Shaw Aulum with pains, violent as from the heavy ftroke of
the keeneft weapon. So inftantaneous was the fatal effect, that it
gave full reafon to imagine it proceeded from poifon. He was all
at once feized with faintings, which continued without intermiffion,
till, on the 21ft of Mohirrim, 1124, being Monday night, he deferted this vain world for that of eternity. He had been, from the
firft inftant of his illnefs, given over, and the princes and ladies of
the haram made continual and loud lamentations round his bed.
It happened one day, that, as Mahummud Moiz ad Dien and
Azeem Oofhawn were fitting near it, the latter, perceiving under
a corner of the pillow a dagger of very exquifite workmanfhip,
took it up to admire the jewels with which it was adorned, and the
water of the blade. Upon his drawing it from the fcabbard, Moiz
ad Dien, jealous of his brother, was feized with a panic. He

A.C. 1712.

ftarted

ftarted up, and retired with fuch precipitation, that he ftruck the turban from his head againft the door of the tent, forgot his flippers at the entrance, and fell down over the ropes. Being affifted to rife and adjuft his drefs by his fervants, who were aftonifhed at his ftrange actions and appearance, he rode off to his tents with all the fpeed and hurry poffible. This occafioned much alarm in the camp, and I, among many others, haftened towards the ᴵdurbar. I met the prince, with his attendants, pufhing on his elephant with frantic hafte; upon obferving which, I endeavoured to pafs unobferved; but he knew me, and fent a meffenger to call me to him. As I had previoufly attached myfelf to Azeem Oofhawn, I did not obey the mandate, but paffed on to the emperor's tents, where I fat down in the guard-room of ²Mahabut Khan, third bukfhi, which was clofe to that of the ameer al amra, who did duty there in perfon. He fent for me, and I found with him Mirza Shaw-nowaz Khan Suffawee. I had before interefted myfelf, at the defire of both, in bringing about a connection between Azeem Oofhawn and the ameer al amra; for which purpofe I had employed Shekh ³Coodderut Oolla as a meffenger, and fometimes my grandfon, ⁴Einaiut Oolla. The ameer al amra now defired me to fend the latter to Azeem Oofhawn, to afk him how he could ferve him on the prefent occafion. I fent him, but he returned with a reply laconic and flight, as if from a nobleman of high rank to the commander of an hundred. It was written in Shekh Cooderut Oolla's (confidant to the prince) own hand, as follows: " As " the Imperial fervants can know no place of fupport but this " court, and moft have already repaired to it, the ameer al amra " may alfo pay his duty, with affurance of a gracious reception,

---

¹ The court of the emperor, or any other perfon in high authority.
² Anglicè, Commanding awe.
³ Anglicè, Providence of God.
⁴ Gift of God.

K   " in

" in the prefence." When the ameer al amra read this, he fhed tears, and faid to me, with much emotion, " You fee the manners " of the prince and his advifers ! Whatever is the will of God, " muft take place. Alas ! the errors of a favourite, unacquainted " with government, often endanger the very exiftence of his " mafter. When fortune frowns on any one, he is fure to do " that which he fhould not." After faying this, he immediately quitted the guard-room, collected his followers, and moved his tents and effects to the quarter of the prince Moiz ad Dien, where he thought his fervices more likely to anfwer his own intereft.

The camp was fo difpofed, that the tents of the emperor were pitched along one bank of the river, and on the other oppofite, thofe of the prince Azeem Oofhawn, at a confiderable diftance from the ' city. The three other princes were encamped nearer to it, but Moiz ad Dien almoft clofe to the walls, and the greateft part of his train occupied the houfes of the neareft ftreets. The influence, riches and power of Azeem Oofhawn, had long raifed againft him the enmity and jealoufy of his brethren, who had, for their general fafety, formed a compact to fupport each other. The ameer al amra had formerly been difgufted at Azeem Oofhawn, for preferring to himfelf, the khankhanan and Mahabut Khan ; from which time he had courted alternately Ruffeh Oofhawn and Jehaun Shaw. On this occafion, he fwore to affift the three brothers in effecting the deftruction of Azeem Oofhawn, and make an equal divifion of the empire and royal treafures among them.

Azeem Oofhawn, already in poffeffion of the Imperial camp, treafury and jewels, had alfo a vaft treafure of his own. Moft of the principal noblemen had joined him, with their followers ; alfo

' Lahore, fituated on the river Rawee, about 200 miles N. of Dhely.

the

the royal artillery. He had, befides, a very confiderable army in his own pay; fo that his brothers, though all leagued againſt him, would have formed but a weak enemy, if he had immediately attacked them. But he acted otherwiſe : he encamped on the plain, keeping the river to his rear, and began to throw up works to defend himſelf, inſtead of courting a general action. Probably this proceeded from tendernefs to his brothers, who he thought would in a few days be deferted by their troops, for want of pay, as they poſſeſſed little or no money; and that they would either willingly acknowledge him emperor, to obtain fettlements, or be delivered into his hands by fome of their pretended friends, to gain his favour.

While he thus flattered himſelf with an eafy conqueſt, the three brothers, by the advice of the ameer al amra, drew all the artillery from the fort of Lahore, and encamped their united forces in one line, making the city their defence to the rear. I happened to be encamped near Mahabut Khan, who immediately, on learning that the ameer al amra had attached himſelf to Moiz ad Dien, fearing to be plundered by his troops, loſt no time in moving off with his family and effects to Azeem Oofhawn, leaving his tents and temporary buildings ſtanding. No fooner was he gone, than the rabble took poſſeſſion of his camp, which they fet on fire, and levelled in an inſtant with the ground. As, on many accounts, I had refolved to embrace the fortunes of Azeem Oofhawn, I would have gone with him; but the camp being a ſtanding one, I had neglected my tents, parted with my carriages, and erected temporary ſheds for my family, fo that I was obliged to remain in an alarming fituation, almoſt alone, for four days. I wiſhed to fend my women to my houfe in the city; but the road to it led through the allied armies, where it was probable they might be infulted or plundered. On the fifth day, I was eafed of my fears, as a ſtrong

efcort

efcort came from the prince Azeem Ooſhawn to conduct to him Shaw-nowaz Khan, Hummeed ad Dien Khan, and ſome other noblemen, who waited for this ſecurity to join him. With them I reached his camp in ſafety, where I happily got poſſeſſion of a ſquare walled about, but without any covering or ſhade: yet even this was as a palace at the time, as it ſerved to protect my women and family. I now paid my reſpects to the prince, who received me gracioufly, conferred upon me many favours, and conſulted me on all important occaſions. Pecuniary rewards, and titles far above my ambition, were allotted for me, and getting ready to paſs the ſeals: at the ſame time, orders were diſpatched to ſummon my ſon, ꞌ Hoſhe-dar Khan, to the preſence, from which he had been detached ſome time before on actual ſervice, with a ſelect force; and, to pay him, a large ſum of money was ſent to me. I refuſed it, however, as I had not people to ſecure its ſafety; and requeſted alſo, that the rank of five thouſand, and title of Azim Khan, which was preparing for me, might not be confirmed, till the prince ſhould become victorious over his enemies, as I had made a vow not to receive them till he ſhould ſit unrivalled on the throne of empire. In fact, I perceived in his weak politics, and want of reſolution, the decline of his cauſe; and ſaw the burning blaſts of ſummer haſtening to deſtroy the ſeaſon of ſpring, as the experienced huſbandman can judge of his harveſts from the changes of the atmoſphere.

When Azeem Ooſhawn had intrenched himſelf, and the three brothers began their approaches to his works on every ſide, his operations became highly blameable in the eyes of the nobility and officers of experience. It appeared to the public, that the ſuperior force dreaded the inferior; and that thoſe who ought to be the

---

ꞌ Anglicè, Endowed with judgment.

befiegers, were now the befieged. Such was the effect, for Azeem Ooſhawn's army grew diſpirited daily, while the enemy's gained ardor every hour, at finding that proſpect of ſuccefs, of which in the beginning they had almoſt defpaired. Our ſoldiers at the works, tired with conſtant watchings and alarms, grew remiſs in their duty: they firſt required unneceſſary aſſiſtance, and at laſt began to defert their poſts. The Imperial artillery, to whom a great ſum of money had been given as a bounty, became difobedient to orders, and even mutinous, in which points they were followed by thoſe of the houſhold. This behaviour made Azeem Ooſhawn change his opinion, that he could purchaſe victory with money only; ſo that he opened his treaſury but ſparingly to the old or new troops, giving, with much reluctance, only one hundred rupees to each trooper who came to offer ſervice with his own horſe, for which ſecurity was alſo demanded. At a criſis of this important nature, but few were tempted to quit the ſervice of their old maſters, for a ſum but inconſiderable in itſelf, and only attainable with ſuch difficulty. In ſhort, the whole camp began to be alarmed, and even the boldeſt officers to feel a dread of the ill conſequences of being cooped up in unneceſſary entrenchments. A cannonade was kept up on both ſides for four days, in each of which the three brothers gained ſome advantage, by advancing their ſtations nearer to the works of the miſguided Azeem Ooſhawn.

On the fifth day, Azeem Ooſhawn moved from his camp in order of battle, and his ſon, the prince 'Mahummud Kerreem, though commander of the advanced corps, was with him, inſtead of being difpatched in front, agreeably to the uſual difpoſition of the line. This was ordered, left, as the enemy were formed into three bodies, one might gain an advantage over him, and another

---

¹ Anglicè, favoured by Mahummud.

intercept

intercept his retreat to the grand line, before he could receive
proper affiftance. Such was the confufion in forming the troops,
that the artillery was quite ufelefsly difpofed, and many pieces, deferted by the men, lay overturned on the ground; while fome of
the chief officers were by their followers left almoft alone, on their
elephants, before the action began. Soleyman Khan Afghan firft
advanced to charge the divifion of Jehaun Shaw, but he was fupported by fo few of his followers, that he could effect nothing, and
was killed in the onfet, before he had reached the enemy's poft.
Jehaun Shaw moved fteadily, in flow order, towards Azeem
Oofhawn, whofe terrified troops began to fall back from around
him. The mifconducted, but truly brave prince, when he faw
his fortune thus unfavourable, though he might have faved himfelf
by mounting a horfe and flying from the field, yet fcorned to owe
his fecurity to difhonour, and would not move from his elephant,
but advanced almoft alone towards Jehaun Shaw. This action,
and fubmitting to be facrificed, was one and the fame. His elephant driver was killed in the inftant, and the few till then remaining friends to his perfon deferted him to a man. He received many
wounds from arrows and fhot, fo that he foon funk down fainting
upon his feat; while his elephant, without a driver, and furious
with pain, ran through the enemy, who purfued him in vain for
fome hours, and during that time the unfortunate prince died of
fatigue and lofs of blood[1]. Sultaun Mahummud Kerreem, his
fon, in the height of the confufion, threw himfelf without hurt
from his elephant, and mounting a horfe brought him by an attendant, efcaped from the field of battle; but only to fuffer, fhortly
after, a worfe fate than dying in action.

---

[1] Ameen ad Dien Sumbullee fays, his elephant rufhed with him into the Rawee, and
was drowned.

It

It happened that, at the beginning of the action, the three princes were drawn up nearly oppofite that part of the camp where I unfortunately had placed my family in a wretched fquare, to which the enemy advanced ftill nearer, as the battle raged, and our troops began to fly. Mahabut Khan, Hummeed ad Dien, and other lords, had in the beginning fent their families acrofs the river to places of fafety, which precaution I was prevented from ufing, by being attendant on Azeem Oofhawn's perfon in the line. The river was about a rocket's flight from the fquare inclofure, and upon the rout of our line, Khan Zummaun, my friend, advifed me, while the enemy's troops were yet employed in fight, to con-duct my women out of danger to the other fide ; at the fame time offering me a boat he had ready for his own fecurity againft purfuit, and a guard of one hundred and fifty perfons, his own followers. Accordingly I placed my wife and daughter in two covered palle-kees, with a fum fomewhat exceeding ' four thoufand gold mhors, a cafket of jewels, betel plate of gold fet with jewels, and other very valuable ornaments belonging to my daughter, defigned for her marriage portion, leaving clothes and every thing elfe to chance. As Providence decreed it, the women's pallekees had juft arrived at a narrow inlet of water, about an arrow's flight from the river, when Azeem Oofhawn's elephant, and Mahummud Kerreem's, were running towards it, purfued by the enemy. I was advanced a little in front to prepare the boat, when fuddenly one of my at-tendants cried out, " Where are you going ? Your honour is " ruined !" I looked behind me, and faw the enemy near my women ; upon which, in a ftate of furious defpair, I haftened back with my grandfon Meer Einaiut Oolla, as Khan Zummaun's people could not reach me in time for my affiftance. We two had juft joined the women, when the rapacious Moguls had begun to

---

' About fix thoufand pounds fterling, reckoning the mhor at fifteen Sicca rupees.

2   plunder ;

plunder; upon which I leaped from my horſe, and ſeizing my wife and daughter by each a hand, ruſhed with them into the rivulet up to their waiſts, and covered the reſt of their perſons with a cloth, drawing my ſword to defend them with my life from further inſult: and, luckily for my honour, their faces were not ſeen by the eyes of a ſtranger. The Moguls, more attentive to gain than ſhedding of blood, after plundering the pallekees and other carriages of every thing, even to the coarſeſt outer coverings, rode off in ſearch of other prey, without attacking me or my attendants, who were hid in different buſhes and hollows. It was during this confuſion, that I ſaw the prince Mahummud Kerreem jump from his elephant, mount a ſervant's horſe, and eſcape. When the alarm was over, and friends and enemies had paſſed by, I was joined by my ſervants from their various ſhelters, and, having replaced my women in the pallekees, returned to my late miſerable dwelling, which had been alſo plundered, even to foot-cloths and carpets. No pillows or ſeats were left us but the bare ground, and no apparel but that drenched in water on our backs; nevertheleſs, I gave grateful thanks to the Almighty for the preſervation of my life and honour, with a ſincere fervor. With the approach of night the confuſion ſlackened, and about nine o'clock all was over, and quiet reſtored. I then ſaid to myſelf, " What is gone, is gone!" and, with a calm mind, recited one hundred and twenty verſes of the ' Meſnavi, beſides an ode applicable to the preſent ſtate of affairs.

The prince Jehaun Shaw, who had taken poſſeſſion of the camp of the vanquiſhed, in the morning ſent covered carriages and other neceſſaries to me, with a gracious meſſage, deſiring that I would come, and pitch my tents near his own. I went accordingly, and was introduced to him. He was ſitting alone, under a canopy,

---

* The Meſnavi is a collection of moral poems, by Molewee Jellal ad Dien Roomi.

near

near his private apartments. When he faw me, he exclaimed, in a joyful voice, " Come, 'Azim Khan, for thy arrival is at a happy " feafon ! I was anxious to fee thee." He then took off the khelaut, which he had put on juft before, and gave it to me, with the munfub of ² fix thoufand, faying, " I have left one degree of rank " to confer upon you on the day of my acceffion to a throne." After which he difmiffed me in a gracious manner, and I took up my ftation near that of ³ Lutfoolla Khan Saduk, his firft minifter.

Jehaun Shaw, who had gained the victory over Azeem Ooſhawn, judging, from the purity of his own intentions, that thoſe of his two brothers and the ameer al amra were equally juft towards him, though fortune had placed all the treafures of the vanquifhed in his power, fcorned to ufe this advantage, contrary to his oath of alliance. He fent the body of Azeem Oofhawn to Moiz ad Dien ; and, when all the plunder of his camp was collected, delivered the whole without delay into the hands of the ameer al amra, who, agreeable to treaty and his own oaths, was to make an impartial divifion of the provinces and treafures between the brothers. This ftrictnefs to his word was the caufe of his ruin. The ameer al amra had privately refolved to feat Moiz ad Dien on the throne without a rival, as he was a weak prince, fond of his pleafures, averfe from bufinefs, and confequently beft fuited to the purpofe of a minifter ambitious of uncontrouled power. With this view, he, on various pretences, delayed making a divifion of the treafure, knowing that the troops of Jehaun Shaw and Ruffeh Oofhawn were already mutinoufly clamorous for the payment of their long arrears, and much

¹ Anglicè, Noble lord; the title which Azeem Oofhawn had offered to confer on him.
² Seven thoufand was properly the higheft rank of nobility. In the decline of the empire, rank of eight and ten thoufand was conferred on powerful minifters.
³ Anglicè, God's mercy. Saduk, Anglicè True, was his family name.

L   difgufted

difgufted at being deprived of the great plunder they had expected from the camp of Azeem Ooſhawn, which had been ſeized from their graſp by the ſtrict diſcipline and honour of Jehaun Shaw. The ameer al amra, with ſeeming attachment, viſited the princes as uſual, and three days paſſed over without their expreſſing diſtruſt at his delay; but their friends clearly ſaw his deſigns, and warned Jehaun Shaw againſt his treachery; offering to prevent their completion, by putting him to death, when he ſhould come next to pay his reſpects. The honourable and noble-minded prince refuſed his aſſent to ſuch propoſals, ſaying, " I cannot conſent to ſuch " diſhonourable and perfidious dealing, for which I ſhould become " heinouſly guilty in the eyes of God, and amongſt men marked " as a traitor and abuſer of power. If empire is decreed me, I " ſhall attain it without trouble; but, if not, of what avail is " treachery, or unjuſt ſhedding of human blood?" At his next viſit, he openly told the ameer al amra the ſuſpicions entertained of his conduct, ſaying, " Even now, perhaps, thy family is dreading " that I may be putting thee to death; which, however politic, I " ſcorn to do by fraud. Riſe then, and go in peace to thine own " houſe." The ameer al amra departed with a ſpeed and precipitation declaring his guilt. The veil, with which he had covered his deſigns, became no longer of uſe; but, inſtead of feeling gratitude to Jehaun Shaw for ſuffering him to live, his enmity increaſed. He now openly avowed his deſtruction, and his intentions to ſupport Moiz ad Dien. Though Jehaun Shaw, virtuous and religiouſly faithful to his word, was generous and juſt in this great action, yet the policy of government will not admit of ſuch conduct being copied as an example of propriety. The world is deceitful, and cannot be commanded but by deceit. The thief, who ſhould wake his ſleeping prey, would only bring ruin on his own head. Virtue and vice being direct oppoſites, cannot exiſt in one dwelling. That, the foundation of which is evil, cannot be ſupported but by evil.   I   When

When the ameer al amra had openly refuſed to perform his agreement, Jehaun Shaw, furious at his behaviour, moved his camp oppoſite to the treacherous nobleman's, and prepared to offer battle without delay. He had juſt now the faireſt proſpect of every ſuccefs; a fine army, attached to his perſon with one mind, good artillery, and a great character among his own and the enemy's troops. But—how uncertain is fortune! This night, by permiſſion of God, a fire broke out in the artillery camp: all the rockets and ſtores of ammunition were deſtroyed, and our army rendered in one inſtant totally uſelefs. The merit of this important miſchief was afterwards claimed by Rajee Khan Maneckporee, who ſaid the fire was purpoſely kindled by his ſpies, for a large bribe. This man was originally of low character and little eſteem, but for this ſervice he was gradually raiſed from a poſt in the artillery, by Moiz ad Dien, to the rank of ſix thouſand. Immediately after this dreadful accident, Rooſtum Dil Khan and Mukhlis Khan haſtened to one of the Imperial powder-works, and obtained ſome freſh ſupplies; but the troops, much diſpirited with their lofs, now became clamorous for money, and began to deſert in great numbers. In ſhort, the ſpirit of the army was changed, ſo that, excepting Lutfoolla Khan, Rooſtum Dil Khan, Mukhlis Khan, and a few others who remained faithful, all the chiefs forfeited their honours, and Jehaun Shaw, plainly perceiving the wavering of his followers, thought it moſt adviſable to prevent worſe conſequences, by putting all to the hazard of an immediate engagement. The next morning at the dawn of day, (being Monday, *anno* 1124,) he formed his A. C. 1712. line, and began a cannonade, which was anſwered by the enemy, and kept up on both ſides till mid-day with equal ſuccefs. At length the fire of Jehaun Shaw began to ſlacken, and his troops to ſeparate on various pretences, as want of water, guarding their baggage, and the like; ſo that near half the army deſerted gradually, in ſpite of the prince's repeated orders to maintain the line.

L 2   Obſerving

Obferving this, he raifed a report that the ameer al amra was killed by a fhot, in confequence of which the enemy were alarmed, and that he fhould immediately charge them, in order to improve fo favourable an event. As he founded the march of victory, his troops believed him, and returned moft of them to their pofts. He then commanded Janee Khan, Rooftum Dil Khan, and Mukhlis Khan, to charge one flank of the enemy, and Lootfulla Khan and others in front, he himfelf heading this laft divifion. It was now about four o'clock, when Jehaun Shaw, without looking behind him to fee how he was fupported by his troops, advanced on the enemy's center with a furious fpeed, where the ameer al amra was ftanding with a few followers, to reconnoitre. Moiz ad Dien had before retired to repofe in his tents. Rooftum Dil Khan and other chiefs rufhed through all oppofition to that quarter, gained the tents, and plundered even the ladies of the haram, among whom were many belonging to the late emperor. Moiz ad Dien, rouzed from fleep, without regarding their fafety, fled to feek his own, undreffed as he was, with the ameer al amra, who was engaged againft Jehaun Shaw in unequal combat, as he had only with him three or four hundred horfe. At this time Ruffeh Oofhawn, who feemingly fupported Moiz ad Dien, but was waiting for an opportunity to deftroy both him and Jehaun Shaw, appeared in the rear of the latter with his whole force. A corps of infantry alfo now oppofed him in front, not only ftopping his charge, but confufing his troops; who, feeing themfelves likely to be furrounded, loft all fpirit, and fled to a man on the right and left, leaving him expofed alone upon his elephant : and he was foon killed by a mufquet fhot. His fon, 'Ferkhundeh Akhter, a prince of moft promifing bodily and mental accomplifhments, who fat behind him, defcended and fought with his fcymetar, till he could ftand no longer, and then fell down dead, covered with wounds. Both the bodies were

' Anglicè, Of fortunate ftar.

carried

carried immediately to the ameer al amra, who ordered the march of victory to be founded. Jehaun Shaw, heroic, juft and benevolent, was all perfect; but ftill, as Providence oppofed his fortune, all his plans turned out directly contrary to their propofed end, and what feemed to promife fuccefs, became the caufe of misfortune Men judge vainly from events, faying, if he had not done fo, thus would or could not have happened: but, alas! in whofe power are events? Our faculties, our ftrength, our thoughts, our friends, are all moved by the inftigation of Providence. Nothing can happen without a caufe, yet our ruin is often brought on by the very caufes which had before occafioned our fuccefs; for God doeth that which pleafeth him, and effecteth that which he hath defigned.

When the day of this fun of royalty had funk in the evening of death, there now remained no other rivals than Moiz ad Dien and Ruffeh Oofhawn. The latter had the firmeft reliance on the attachment and oaths of the ameer al amra, who, during the life of the late emperor, had been fupported by him in the ftrongeft manner againft the khankhanan. He alfo had honoured him, at his own requeft, by the appellation of uncle, and 'exchange of turbans; fo that he now hoped, as one fovereign feemed to be his choice, that it might reft upon him, in preference to his elder brother. On this account, he had refolved to wait as a fpectator of the ftruggle, till the fall of one of his rivals, and then to rufh upon the furvivor, while flufhed with victory, and unguarded againft a new enemy. This defign he now communicated to his followers, and defired them to fupport him in an immediate attack on Moiz ad Dien; but they would not confent, either through fear or treachery, pretending that the dawn of morning was more favour-

---

' The exchange of turbans, among the orientals, is the moft facred pledge of friend-fhip, and any breach of it, after fuch ceremony, regarded with horror.

able than the prefent inftant; fo that the prince was obliged to
ftop, and wait their pleafure. He fpent the night under arms,
with fleeplefs impatience for the return of day; but fome of his
falfe advifers communicated his plan to the ameer al amra, and
promifed to affift in the deftruction of their patron.

Juft as the morning was beginning to appear, Ruffeh Oofhawn
advanced filently towards the enemy, hoping to furprize them;
but, before he had reached their camp, the commanding officer of
his artillery, either through treachery or ignorance, fired a gun
towards the quarter of Moiz ad Dien, which roufed his fleeping
troops. The alarm was immediately founded, and the enemy's
cannon foon began to play furioufly. Who now would ftand to
fupport Ruffeh Oofhawn? The greateft number of his followers
fled in confufion to the right and left, while Buddukfhee, a chief
in whom he had repofed the greateft confidence, and whom he had
faved from being put to death by his father, whom he had raifed
to honours, and fupported with a liberality unbounded, having
privately agreed with the ameer al amra, ungratefully turned his
arms againft him at this inftant. The unhappy prince was in a
fhort time left alone, furrounded by his enemies on every fide; but
truly brave and fpirited, regarding the honour and reputation of
the family of Timur, notwithftanding his delicacy and feeming
effeminate foftnefs, he threw himfelf from his elephant, and, drawing the fabre of glory from the fcabbard of honour, fought fingly
on foot againft thoufands of affailants. But what could he effect,
more than fell one life at the expence of many? He was foon
hewed down with repeated wounds, and refigned his breath to him
who gave it. May the Almighty fhew mercy to his foul! We are
from God, and to him we muft return.

Such courage, I muft with juftice remark, never appeared among
the defcendants of Timur, as fhewn by the offspring of Aulumgeer;

nor

nor do the various hiftories I have read, record the like gallant oppofition of a prince fingly againft numbers. True valour is proved
in the extremity of danger; but it is eafy to affume the appearance
of courage in the day of fafety.

Moiz ad Dien Jehaundar Shaw, by the affiftance of Providence
alone, now founded the march of victory and unrivalled empire.
He permitted the mangled bodies of his martyred and more worthy
brothers to be kept three days on the field of battle, expofed to
public view. They were afterwards conveyed to Dhely, and interred
without ceremony or pomp, in the maufoleum of the emperor
Humaioon, the general receptacle of the murdered princes of the
Imperial family. The maufoleums which they had erected for
themfelves, near the tombs of their favourite faints, of marble,
jafper, and other rich ftones, were beftowed on the minions of
Lall Koor, a public dancer, and miftrefs to the weak Jehaundar
Shaw.

Be it known to thofe of enlightened underftandings, and to the
acquainted with the ufages of the world, that if, in the relation of
the affairs of my liege and hereditary lord, the emperor Moiz ad
Dien Jehaundar Shaw, fome obfervations and expreffions fhould
efcape my pen, contrary to refpect, and the examples of the hifto-
riographers of princes, they will not proceed from difaffection or
a prejudiced mind. I know they are improper from the pen of a
fervant, and God forgive me! but by them I mean no difaffection
to his perfon, or difrefpect to the family of Timur; no vent of my
own fpleen; no view to flatter a fucceffor, by difparaging his rival,
nor malicious abufe for the neglect or difappointment I may have
fuffered during this reign. I fwear by God, and God is a facred
witneffer of oaths, that I loved him as my fovereign; but, as it
was incumbent on me to record the actions of the reigning prince,
good or bad, wife or foolifh, in public and private, if they were,

without

without one exception, all unworthy, what can I fay, as a faithful writer? Let it be remembered, that I was nourifhed for fifty years under the benignant fhadow of the great and glorious emperor Aulumgeer. How fad the alteration I now beheld! Of this man, this wretched idiot, oppofite to him in every quality, fucceeding to the very fame empire, fitting on the very fame throne, and the actions he did, what can I fay, or in what terms paint the difgraces they fuffered by his acceffion?—I had beheld upon the throne an emperor. Warmth of expreffion operates in advice: the friends to the ¹Imaums, from the ardor of their loyalty to the houfe of Ali, heightened their ftyle, and reprefented with all the eloquence of zeal (for which they have been ever praifed by good men) that the opprefled might draw the fword againft a worthlefs tyrant. But I only mean a warning to the family of Timur; for the head of which, let his character be what it may, if I hefitate to facrifice my life, may I be numbered with traitors, and abhorred by my friends!

When Jehaundar Shaw, by the intrigues and fupport of the ameer al amra Zoolfeccar Khan, had triumphed over his three brothers, and afcended the throne of empire without the fear or dread of a competitor, all the cuftoms of time were changed. He was in himfelf a weak man, effeminately careful of his perfon, fond of eafe, indolent, and totally ignorant of the arts of government. He had alfo blemifhes and low vices unworthy of royalty, and un-known among his illuftrious anceftors. He made the vaft empire of Hindoftan an offering to the foolifh whims of a public courtezan, which tortured the minds of worthy fubjects loyal to his family. The relations, friends and minions of the miftrefs, ufurped abfolute

¹ The two chief Imaums were the fons of Ali, by the daughter of Mahummud, and were put to death by the caliph Maweeah, one by poifon, and the other in battle, with all their children except one, from whom defcended the other ten Imaums, and the race of Syeds, fo highly refpected among the Mahummedans.

authority

authority in the ftate; and high offices, great titles, and unreafonable grants from the Imperial domains, were fhowered profufely on beggarly muficians. [1] Two corores of rupees annually were fettled for the houfhold expences of the miftrefs only, exclufive of her cloaths and jewels. The emperor frequently rode with her in a chariot through the markets, where they purchafed, agreeable to whim, fometimes jewels, gold, filks, and fine linen; at others, greens, fruits, and the moft trifling articles. A woman named [2] Zohera, keeper of a green-ftall, one of Lall Koor's particular friends, was promoted to a high rank, with a fuitable jaghire, and

[1] About two millions fterling.

[2] The celebrated Nizam al Mulluk, who at this time lived a very retired life at Dhely, was one day paffing in a pallekee, with only a few attendants, when, in a narrow ftreet, he was met by Zohera, who was riding on an elephant, with a great train of fervants. The nizam endeavoured to get out of the way; but, notwithftanding this, Zohera's fervants were infolent to his attendants, and, as fhe paffed by, fhe exclaimed, " Are you the fon of the blind man?" This enraged the nizam, who commanded his people to pull her from her elephant; which they did, with rudenefs. She complained to the miftrefs, who prevailed on the weak Jehaundar to take notice of it, and command Zoolfeccar Khan to punifh the nizam. The nizam had fufpected this to happen, and had informed the minifter of the affair. When Jehaundar Shaw fpoke to him, he was anfwered, that, to punifh the nizam for having corrected an infolent upftart, would enrage all the nobility, who would confider the honour of the order as hurt by any affront to the nizam. Jehaundar, upon this, did not enforce his commands.

Upon Jehaundar Shaw's premoting one of his miftrefs's relations, a mufician, to a high rank, Zoolfeccar Khan, ameer al amra, out of fneer, demanded of the new-made lord, as a fee for putting his feal of office to the patent, one thoufand fmall tabors. The mufician complained to Lall Koor, his patronefs, of the indignity offered him; and fhe told the emperor, infifting that he fhould reprimand the ameer al amra. Jehaundar Shaw accordingly reproached the minifter, who ironically replied, that, as mufic was the beft recommendation with his majefty for promotion, he had afked the tabors to deliver out to perfons of family, that they might, by practifing upon them, qualify themfelves for high office, and fucceed as well as their inferiors, the muficians. Jehaundar Shaw felt the force of the fatire, and, being afraid of his minifter, withdrew the patent.

M

her

her relations exalted to the emperor's favour, which they ufed to promote the interefts of the courtiers, for large bribes : nor did the nobility decline their patronage, but forgetting their honour, and facrificing decency to the prefent advantage, eagerly flocked to pay adoration to the royal idols, whofe gates were more crowded with equipages in general than thofe of the Imperial palace, fo that to pafs through the ftreet where they refided was a matter of difficulty, by reafon of the throng.   To do them juftice, many of them had generous minds, and performed various good actions in the ufe of their influence at court.   The ridiculous jaunts of the emperor and his miftrefs at laft grew to fuch a pitch, that on a certain night, after fpending the day in debauchery, and vifiting different gardens near the city, in company with Zohera the herb-woman, they re- tired to the houfe of one of her acquaintance who fold fpirits, with which they all became intoxicated.   After rewarding the woman with a large fum, and the grant of a village, they returned in a drunken plight to the palace, and all three fell afleep on the road. On their arrival, Lall Koor was taken out by her women; but the emperor remained fleeping in the chariot, and the driver, who had fhared in the jollity of his royal mafter, without examining the machine, carried it to the ftables.   The officers of the palace, after waiting till near morning for his arrival, on finding that the miftrefs had entered her apartments without the emperor, were alarmed for his fafety, and fent to her to enquire concerning his fituation.   She defired them immediately to examine the coach, where they found the wretched prince faft afleep in the arms of Zohera, at the diftance of nearly two miles from the palace.   This fcandalous event afforded matter of offence to all good fubjects, but of mirth and laughter to the weak Jehaundar and his abandoned favourites.   He after this ftill more expofed his vices to the public, often, as he paffed through the ftreets, feizing the wives and daugh- ters of the lower tradefmen.   Once a week, according to the vulgar

fuperftition,

superstition, he bathed with Lall Koor, concealed only by a single cloth, in the fountain of the [1] Lamp of Dhely, in hopes that this ceremony would promote pregnancy. Happy was the day in which he was bathed in his own blood! The mistress had the insolence to abuse the princess [2] Zebe al Nissa, daughter of the emperor Aulumgeer, and aunt to Jehaundar Shaw, with expressions so vile as were unbecoming the meanest person. This princess had neglected to pay compliments to her, which she received from other ladies of rank, and Lall Koor, enraged at this, teized the emperor to reprove his aunt, and oblige her to shew attention towards her; but all was vain. However, he so far complied with her unreasonable entreaties, that he left off visiting the princess, and declined going to an entertainment she had prepared for him, without inviting Lall Koor. How shall I relate all his follies? The abovementioned are sufficient to shew the sad changes of affairs, public and private. His other indecencies are too unworthy of record to relate.

The ameer al amra, Zoolfeccar Khan, feater, nay even creator of emperors, with such an image of humanity in his hands, became absolute, and so proud, that [3] Pharaoh and Shudad could not have obtained admission to his threshold. He studied to ruin the most ancient families, inventing pretences to put them to death, or disgrace them, that he might plunder their possessions. Unhappy was the person he suspected to be rich, as wealth and vexatious accusations always accompanied each other. He established such exactions and abuses as no prior age had beheld, and by which now he is alone remembered. He took enormous emoluments and revenues for himself, while he disposed of money to others with a

[1] A celebrated fakeer so entitled.
[2] Anglicè, Ornament of the sex.
[3] Pharaoh, and a king of Yemmum, or Arabia Felix.

hand

hand fo fparing, that even his own creatures felt fevere poverty with empty titles, for he never allowed jaghires to any. The minds of high and low, rich and poor, near or diftant, friends or ftrangers, were turned againft him, and wifhed his deftruction. Hindoos and Muffulmans agreed in praying to Heaven for the fall of his power, night and day. Often does the midnight figh of the widow ruin the riches of an hundred years.

Kokultafh Khan, fofter-brother to the emperor, and brought up with him from his childhood, was honoured with the title of Khan Jehaun. His wife, daughter, and whole family, alfo poffeffed great influence with the emperor, and claimed from him performance of a promife he had made to them of the vizurut. At the fame time, they and their adherents combined to work the overthrow of the ameer al amra. With this view, all their relations and dependants were raifed to high rank; and a great number of the nobility, dif-treffed by the pride and rapacity of Zoolfeccar Khan, joined their party. They infinuated to the emperor, that the ameer al amra entertained defigns too ambitious for a fubject, to attain which he would dare to fhed the blood of princes; that he had already deter-mined on a revolution, and either to feize the throne for himfelf, or, if he found that too dangerous, to beftow it on ꞌAli Tibbar, or another of the confined princes, more favourable to his will than his majefty.

The weak Jehaundar, unendowed with the leaft judgment or cou-rage, was alarmed almoft to madnefs with the frightful picture of his own fituation; but he had not firmnefs to oppofe the dreaded evils, nor fenfe to keep his fears fecret. The intrigues of Kokul-tafh Khan foon became evident to the whole court, and only ferved to awaken the vigilance of the ameer al amra, who took meafures

----

ꞌ The only furviving fon of Azim Shaw, fon of the emperor Aurungzebe.

for

for his own fafety, by removing his enemies. Rooftum Dil Khan, Mukhlis Khan, and fome others, were put to death, and a great number of the nobility laid under confinement on various pretences. The family of the late ¹ khankhanan was reduced fo low as to want the common neceffaries of life. In fhort, the difpofition of the ameer al amra changed altogether from gentlenefs to the higheft pitch of tyranny, fo that he now punifhed with cruelty the perfons who had years before knowingly, or otherwife, given him the flighteft caufes of offence. I, who had differed with him in opinions during the life of Bedar Bukht, and frequently warned the late emperor againft his afpiring views, had alfo been the friend and confidant of his mortal enemy the khankhanan, and of a different party in the late ftruggle, had not a hope of efcaping from his hands, or thofe of Jehaundar Shaw, who had commanded me to be fearched for, and put to death. Thinking it in vain to attempt concealment in Lahore, I had written the following verfes, and fent them to him by my grandfon, Meer Einaiut Oolla, who was much in his favour.

" My anceftors were attached to ² Ali without views of gain. I " am of the family of Ali; thou art the ³ Zoolfeccar of ⁴ Hyder. " Remember, I have no chief but thee. I repent of my faults in " fome degree, and am come afhamed to thy tribunal. Though I " am meaner than words can exprefs, yet I am of the ⁵ family of " which thou art head. Thou art now the guardian of our ho- " nour: look not at me, but upon our mutual anceftors."

¹ The celebrated Monauim Khan.
² The fon-in-law of Mohammud. Here it means Azeem al Shawn.
³ A two-bladed fword of Ali's.
⁴ A title given to Ali.
⁵ A fyed, or defcendant from the prophet's daughter Fatima, by Ali.

At

At firft he did not trouble himfelf to open the paper, upon which I fent a fecond time, when he perufed it with attention, and defired the meffenger to call me to him; but I did not comply with his invitation, to which I anfwered, that he had prevailed with promifes of fafety on many to vifit him, and afterwards confined or put them to death; that if fuch was his defign towards me, there was no occafion to ufe art, as I would of my own accord put on my fhroud, and come prepared for the worft before him. To this he anfwered, by folemn oaths, that he meant no injury towards me; fo that I was fatisfied, and went to vifit him without dread. He received me in his private apartment, to which I was admitted armed, as ufual, and he rofe from his mufnud to falute me, behaving every way with much kindnefs, and more than I expected; after which he difmiffed me, with affurances of protection. He the fame day afked the emperor's pardon for me, which was immediately paffed; but his majefty obferved, that though he forgave, he would not on any account employ me in his fervice. The ameer al amra too made me promife, that I would not accept of any office in the ftate, otherwife than through his patronage. I complied with his defire without regret, as, independent of the obligations I owed to him, there was no temptation left to court employment in a ftate which had in fact no head; for the miniftry was a collection of petty tyrants, and abufers of power.

During the nine months in which Jehaundar Shaw, like an embryo, lay in the womb of empire, I did not attempt to procure an office, but lived in perfect retirement, except that I now and then unavoidably paid a vifit to the ameer al amra, who would frequently afk my advice in public affairs, which I gave him to the extent of my underftanding.

In the height of this power and authority, (while the claim of *I am, and no one elfe,* was gaining ftrength,) all at once a report was heard that the prince Ferokhſere, ſon to the martyred Azeem Ooſhawn, had marched from Bengal towards Bahar, intending to revenge his father's death, and ſeize the throne. Jehaundar Shaw and the ameer al amra, though they feigned to diſbelieve the intelligence, and deſpiſe the attempt, yet in their hearts were ſtruck with dread. Great numbers of the Imperial ſervants wiſhed ſecretly for the ſucceſs of the rebellion. While the ameer al amra was fortunate, he ſaw affairs in a proper light: while at Lahore, he had repeatedly adviſed Jehaundar Shaw not to remain more than a week in Dhely, but to proceed to Agra, and, if neceſſary, to the eaſtern provinces, as the dread of his power would not be impreſſed fully in the breaſts of his ſubjects, while Ferokhſere refuſed to pay allegiance. Jehaundar Shaw, on his arrival at Dhely, faſcinated by the various luxuries it afforded, forgot the advice of his miniſter, and choſe to remain, indulging himſelf in low pleaſures, moving only from palace to palace, and garden to garden. Kokultaſh Khan and his party perſuaded him that the ameer al amra had excited this rebellion, and engaged privately with Ferokhſere, to whom he would deliver his majeſty a priſoner, ſhould he prevail on him to march from the capital. Theſe ideas ſerved to increaſe the fears of the weak Jehaundar Shaw. He would often exclaim, " I did not " kill Azeem Ooſhawn: it was the ameer al amra, who muſt now " go and anſwer the claims of his ſon, for ſatisfaction. What " have I to do with the buſineſs?" The other plans of an emperor, who was thus overcome by fear, may eaſily be gueſſed, and need no explanation. The ameer al amra, offended at the diſtruſts of his maſter, did not attend as he ought to buſineſs, but employed his time alſo in pleaſure, and forwarding his own immediate intereſt.

Syed Abdoolla Khan Bareah, and his brother Houſſein Ali Khan, had gained great honour by their behaviour in the ſervice of Azim

Shaw,

Shaw, after whofe death they had attached themfelves to Azeem Oofhawn, by whom they were honoured, the former with the government of Allahabad, and the latter of the province of Bahar. During the late contefts for the empire, they had, for their own fafety and that of the country, expended, without orders, confiderable fums of the Imperial revenues in the maintenance of extraordinary troops, which had offended Jehaundar Shaw. On his acceffion to the throne, he appointed Rajee Khan Maneckporee to the government of Allahabad, who fent one of his relations, with a confiderable force, to take poffeffion ; but he was oppofed, defeated, and driven back by Abdoolla Khan. Ferokhfere's rebellion juft then arifing, the ameer al amra thought it advifable to difpatch an Imperial firmaun, approving Abdoolla Khan's conduct, and confirming him in his government, difclaiming alfo any affent to the attempts to remove him. Abdoolla Khan pretended gratitude and obedience for the royal favours, in order to avoid farther trouble from the court, but which he had refolved to ferve no longer than he found neceffary. When Ferokhfere arrived in Bahar, he was immediately joined by Syed Houffein Ali Khan, who was faithfully attached to him, as the fon of his patron Azeem Oofhawn. The court of Dhely weakly imagined, that Abdoolla Khan would ftop the progrefs of the prince at Allahabad. Firmauns of encouragement, and great promifes, were difpatched to purchafe his loyalty, inftead of armies to fecure it. While the rebellion was daily gathering force, the emperor's minifters, divided againft each other, were undetermined how to act. Kokultafh Khan refufed to take the command of an army, if the ameer al amra remained at Dhely, pretending that the emperor was not fafe in his hands ; and the latter did not think it proper to quit the court, where, in his abfence, fuch a dangerous rival muft poffefs the whole power. Jehaundar Shaw did not dare to think, much lefs to fix, whom he fhould entruft with the command of the army ; for fo great was

his

his fear, that one day, when the daughter of Kokultaſh Khan, preſuming on her familiarity, inſiſted that her father ſhould be declared vizier, and the ameer al amra be ſent from Dhely, he replied with terror, " Hold your peace, or [1] he will put us all to " death in an inſtant."

At laſt it was reſolved that [2] Aiz ad Dien, eldeſt ſon of Jehaundar Shaw, ſhould march at the head of an army againſt the rebels, under the tutelage of Khaja Houſſein, Khan Downan, ſon-in-law to Kokultaſh Khan, a weak man, who never, unleſs in dreams, had ſeen a ſhot fired. The troops who marched with him did not amount to ſix thouſand, though there were among the officers many ameers of the higheſt rank. On his arrival at Agra, he was joined by Iauts, Rajapootes, and great numbers of other rabble; alſo many Fojedaurs, who covered ground, but were no better than droves of cattle to devour proviſions ; however, he had with him a fine train of artillery. From Agra, Aiz ad Dien marched without delay to [3] Etawa, and from thence to [4] Cudjwa, where Ferokhſere had arrived with the two Syeds, and near ſeventy thouſand horſe and foot, moſtly adventurers, who ſerved from the hope of benefiting themſelves by a revolution.

The two camps being thus near, on the 29th of Showal, early in the morning, Syed Abdoolla Khan and others advanced to re-connoitre the enemy's poſition. This brought on a ſkirmiſh, and afterwards a cannonade on both ſides, which continued till night, without much execution ; but Khan Dowran, a perfect ſtranger to

[1] Meaning the ameer al amra.
[2] Elder brother of the late, and uncle to the preſent emperor.
[3] A large town on the Jumna, thirty coſs to the eaſtward of Agra.
[4] A conſiderable town in the diſtrict of Kora, where Aurungzebe and Sultan Shujah formerly engaged.

war,

war, was much alarmed at the dangers of his new profeffion. He thought he fhould do the ftate moft fervice by faving the prince from (as he conceived) inevitable deftruction. Accordingly, un- known to his officers, about midnight he fled with him in a wo- man's covered pallekee, ftopping not till he arrived at Agra, from whence he difpatched to court accounts of his gallant fervice, and zealous care of the heir-apparent. The officers of his army, in the morning, finding their chief had fled, laid afide all thoughts of refiftance, and each provided for his own fafety. Moft went over to the fervice of Ferokhfere, and the remainder returned precipi- tately towards Agra. Syed Abdoolla Khan would not allow them to be purfued, and, what has often perplexed my underftanding to account for, advifed Ferokhfere to halt fome time in the camp of the fugitives, inftead of following his fuccefs with rapidity. The news of the defeat reaching Dhely, threw the court into fuch con- fufion, that no other plan was at firft refolved on, than to wait the enemy's approach in the vicinity of the city, and hazard all in one engagement, as it was expected time would not allow of more diftant operations. Accordingly, Rajee Khan was ordered with the Imperial artillery to ' Feridabad, where ground was chofen for the general camp, and preparations made for the emperor's march.

As foon as it became known that Ferokhfere had not advanced beyond the field of battle, Jehaundar Shaw altered his refolution of remaining at Dhely, and began his march towards Agra. On his arrival there, the ameer al amra opened the royal treafures, which had been for ages laid up, difpofing of money, jewels, plate, and valuable effects, to the amount of two corores of rupees, among the troops, who now were feventy thoufand horfe, and foot without number. Moft of them too were veteran foldiers, but little affected

---

' About three cofs from the city.

to the royal caufe, as they had experienced flights in the days of peace, and knew this profufe bounty to proceed only from the neceffity of the times. The Imperial army encamped at firft near the gardens of Dehera; but, upon intelligence arriving that Ferokhfere had advanced to Eatimadpore, near the river, intending to crofs, it was thought advifable to move along the oppofite bank to prevent him. Both armies remained a week thus, in fight of each other; and people of judgment decided, in their own minds, that victory would be to that prince who fhould firft crofs and attack his rival.

On the night of the 13th of Zeekaud, intelligence was received A. H. 1124.
A. C. 1712. that the Syeds had, by a countermarch of twenty miles, gained the ford of Gaow Ghaut, and croffed the river with their advanced corps and all the artillery; alfo that Ferokhfere, with his whole army, intended to follow the next day. I was prefent when this news was brought to the ameer al amra, who, on hearing it, was vifibly affected and alarmed, as were all the nobility then prefent in his train. Orders of march were iffued for the next morning, to meet the enemy, whofe camp was, by the late manoeuvre, removed ten cofs diftant. Jehaundar Shaw moved accordingly, but halted before he had fight of the enemy, encamping on the broken ground and hollow ways on the banks of the Jumna. This difpirited the troops, who judged that their generals had chofen a ftrong pofition, more from fear of a fudden attack, than proper caution and judgment of the ground. The next morning, however, the Imperial army continued the march to Secundra, and the day after to Gaow Ghaut, where the enemy's troops were ftill croffing, and Ferokhfere had not as yet come to this fide. The ameer al amra, with a number of nobility, advanced in front to reconnoitre the pofition of the enemy, as did alfo the emperor, when he arrived with the main army. The Syeds, notwithftanding their inferior force, drew up

N 2

to

to receive them, but the ameer al amra chofe to defer taking advantage of his prefent fituation, as it was now late in the afternoon, and the fall of night, during an action, would create much confufion and diforder.   With this idea, he chofe to encamp on the banks of a rivulet which ran between him and the enemy.

Early in the morning of the next day, which began with heavy clouds and rain, I went to vifit the ameer al amra, who was juft come from the emperor's tents, and preparing to take fome refrefhment; upon which, I afked my difmiffion, and returned to my own tents, intending to fleep.   By this time the clouds had difperfed, and the fun fhone very bright.   A little after mid-day, I was alarmed by the drums beating to arms, and a confufed noife, when running to my door, I faw the ameer al amra mounting his elephant with great hafte, and undreffed; upon which I got ready my attendants, about forty perfons, and followed him with all poffible fpeed.   Upon my arrival, he was ftanding upon elevated ground, looking round him.   I afked what had caufed the alarm, when he replied, that the enemy were drawing out their line, feemingly with intentions to cannonade.   Our troops now haftened to form, the ameer al amra in front, and upon his right Kokultafh Khan.   In the center ftood the emperor, Jehaundar Shaw, attended by Rajee Khan, with the royal artillery.   To the left were the troops of Mortuzza Khan Bukfhi, and many other amràs.   The enemy's army advanced flowly till within reach of cannon-fhot, when they played upon us with their artillery and rockets, which were anfwered with great fury by Rajee Khan.   Every one knows that, after an engagement is once begun, it is impoffible for a fingle perfon to fee more of the operations than thofe on the immediate fpot of his own poft; how then can I fay, I diftinctly viewed every change of two lines covering ground of miles in extent?   An author once read to Aurungzebe a long account of one

3   of

of his battles with Dara Shekkoh. The emperor obferved at the conclufion, that he muft certainly have been upon a high mountain during the engagement, which he had feen fo minutely, as he himfelf, though commanding the line, and mounted on an elephant, did not perceive one-third of the particulars he had defcribed. In fhort, I fhall only relate what I faw. After a cannonade of fome time, I faw two bodies from the enemy's line charge our's, one with a red, and the other with a green ftandard. The former was the corps of Raja Jubbeeleh Ram, and the latter of Syed Houffein Ali Khan. Obferving that our right flank was much expofed, I remarked it to the ameer al amra, who immediately difpatched orders for Abdul Summud Khan to move with the miftrefs's troops to that quarter. The firft body of the enemy charged directly on Kokultafh Khan, and the other pufhing through the line of our artillery, which was deferted as it approached, attacked the center, in which was Jehaundar Shaw. Our troops fell back upon the camp, and great confufion took place, as the men, elephants and horfes, became entangled among the ropes of tents, carriages and baggage. Numbers fled, but the ameer al amra remained firm, and the enemy was kept long at a ftand by his gallantry and fteadinefs; but he was ill-fupported, though Syed Houffein Ali Khan fell wounded in the field, and Jubbeeleh Ram was not more fuccefsful in his charge on Kokultafh Khan. It was now about five o'clock, when affairs were thus doubtful; but juft then Syed Abdoolla Khan, with a great body, charged Jehaundar Shaw, who ftood with his troops, already alarmed, fome diftance in the rear of the ameer al amra. They fcarce waited to be attacked, but broke their line, and fled in confufion on all fides, while the women's elephants, thofe of the jewel office and treafury, ran here and there, carrying diforder along with them. Jehaundar Shaw haftily joined the corps of Kokultafh Khan, and was purfued by the enemy, who thus forced him between two fires, Ferokhfere

having

having now come to the affiftance of Jubbeeleh Ram, who had renewed the attack in front. Kokultafh Khan was killed after a
fhort ftruggle, his troops difperfed, and Jehaundar Shaw difap-
peared from his elephant. This made the rout general, and only
the ameer al amra kept his ground. When he could hear no tidings
of the emperor, and it became dark, he retifed flowly to Shaw
Gunge, near the city, where he remained till midnight, difpatching
meffengers on all fides in fearch of his fovereign, with the hopes,
if he could be found, of rallying the troops, and making one more
effort the next day; but all in vain. Jehaundar Shaw could not be
found; upon which he thought proper to provide for his own
fafety, and marched away towards Dhely. Thus, in the fpace of
a few hours, was this government deftroyed, and another poffeffed
of abfolute authority. The robe of empire graced the auguft perfon of Ferekhfere, who founded the joyful march of triumph.

Though I was not in the fervice of any one, and had no enmity
to either party, yet I remained in the field till the ameer al amra had
retired, when thinking it beft to provide for my own fafety, I
entered the city with about a hundred perfons who fought my protection, and retired to one of my own gardens, where I enjoyed
perfect repofe from my fatigues. In the morning, I wrote to Syed
Abdoolla Khan, with whom I was formerly on terms of friendfhip,
expreffing my defire of leave to vifit him, and be introduced to the
new emperor. He replied to my letter with much kindnefs, and I
paid my compliments to him as he paffed by my dwelling the following day, when he carried me with him to his own houfe. The
emperor Ferokhfere entered the city the next morning, to pray in
public at the tomb of Akber, on his return from whence I was
allowed to pay him my refpects. Syed Abdoolla Khan marched
towards Dhely the day after, and chofe to take me with him,
which I did not think proper to decline. As yet, it was not certainly

tainly known to what quarter Jehaundar Shaw and the ameer al amra had fled. Affud ad Dowlah, father to the latter, was in the command of Dhely, and had in his power the confined princes. It was apprehended that the ameer al amra would retreat to Dekkan with his mafter, but he not finding that prince, thought proper to go to Dhely. Jehaundar Shaw, who had fhaved his beard and whifkers to prevent being known, arrived a fhort time before the ameer al amra, at the palace of Affud ad Dowlah. This was foon known throughout the city; upon which the friends to the family of Azeem Oofhawn furrounded the houfe, and demanded the delivery of the royal fugitive into their charge. Affud ad Dowlah was obliged to confine him, to fupprefs their clamours. Making a virtue of neceffity, he wrote a petition to Ferokhfere, implying, that he had imprifoned Jehaundar in his own houfe, and waited the Imperial orders concerning his difpofal. In return, firmauns were difpatched applauding his conduct, forgiving all paft offences, and continuing him in the vizarut, with Syed Abdoollah Khan as his deputy, to whofe care Jehaundar Shaw was for the prefent to be entrufted. All thefe gracious affurances fatisfied Affud ad Dowlah, and had fuch an effect on the ameer al amra, his fon, that he thought it beft to remain at Dhely, and wait the emperor's mercy, which he hoped would fpare his forfeited life and fortune.

When Ferokhfere arrived near Dhely, he commanded Affud ad Dowlah and his fon to be brought into his prefence. They were both received with the honours due to their high rank; after which, the former was allowed to return in fafety to his own houfe, but the latter was led to a private tent, and, after a few queftions had been afked him, he was ftrangled, as a punifhment for his crimes, and an example to others. His body was afterwards tied with the head downwards on an elephant, together with that of Jehaundar Shaw, who had been put to death in prifon, and expofed in the

7 new

new emperor's train, when he made his triumphant entry to the palace; after which, both bodies were thrown into the ſtreet, before the great moſque, and remained ſome days a ſpectacle to the mob. The eſtates of the father and ſon were confiſcated, and their family, which had filled for above two hundred years the higheſt offices of the ſtate, was thus in an inſtant levelled with the duſt, and, like that of ¹ Bermekee, totally ruined. Some other traitors were alſo puniſhed with death, which impreſſed the ſubject with reſpect for government, and proved that however, for a time, treaſons might be attended with ſucceſs, at length the proſperity of the houſe of Timur would be prevalent over all oppoſition.

Such is the firſt beaming of the heaven-given fortune of his majeſty, which, by divine bleſſing, is aſcending to the zenith of glory and renown. Praiſe be to God, by whoſe favour the con-cluſion of my book is auſpicious! and mercy upon the choſen of mankind, Mahummud, his deſcendants, his friends and followers, for evermore! Amen.

¹ Known in Europe by the name of Barmecides, as mentioned in the life of Haroon al Raſheed, in the Hiſtory of the Caliphs.

F I N I S.

For EU product safety concerns, contact us at Calle de José Abascal, 56–1°,
28003 Madrid, Spain or eugpsr@cambridge.org.

www.ingramcontent.com/pod-product-compliance
Ingram Content Group UK Ltd.
Pitfield, Milton Keynes, MK11 3LW, UK
UKHW030856150625
459647UK00021B/2790